Igniting the Blue Flame

ANSWERING THE CALL TO LEADERSHIP

BILL WEBB

The Blue Flame Project, LLC.
703 Chaucer Court
Southlake, TX 76092

Visit Our Website at www.theblueflameproject.com

ISBN 13: 978-0-9791445-0-9

Published by The Blue Flame Project, LLC,
Southlake, Texas.

Cover and Interior Design by Nevine Younes,
Exarte Design, Inc.

Printed in the United States of America

THE BLUE FLAME
PROJECT™

IGNITING PASSION FOR LEADERSHIP™

Table of Contents

SUCCESS IS NOT THE RESULT OF
SPONTANEOUS COMBUSTION. YOU
MUST FIRST SET YOURSELF ON FIRE.

FRED SHERRO

Introduction

I

T'S HARD TO IGNORE FIRE. It is one of the basic tools of human culture and its discovery still ranks as one of our most significant accomplishments. Used responsibly, it embodies the power to transform through its energy, light new paths, prepare food and share warmth.

Leaders face a similar opportunity. Practiced with good care, leadership can become like the blue flame that burns hot and steady at the center of a fire. When they accept the challenge, leaders become catalysts for positive change, calling those around them into action with their attitude and example.

The amount of information available on the subject of leadership is surpassed only by the difficulty in consistently applying leadership principles in our daily lives. In fact, I believe there truly are very few new concepts when it comes to how we lead. There may be a new twist here or there, but the basics remain the same. Why?

Because basic leadership principles are common sense—plain and simple. We are not talking about rocket science. We are talking about applying the same values, practices, and ideas to others that we want applied to us.

But if leadership is so straight forward, why is the world full of managers instead of leaders? Because it is easier to manage than lead. Because there is a significant difference in managing and leading and many people don't understand that difference. They don't understand how leadership is so much more effective in today's ever-changing business environment.

Managing is an assignment and leadership is a choice. Managing is what happens while you and your people are in the room together while leadership is what occurs after you leave the room. Managing resembles a one-way street and is often exercised in response to problems, while leadership is a four-way intersection navigated daily. When you make the decision to lead, it comes with the responsibility to continue learning and growing in your role.

Over the past decade, I have had the opportunity to work with many organizations around the country as they endeavor to energize their people through leadership and executive development programs. The results are very rewarding not only for the people I work with, but for me as well.

My role is part motivation and part training. My goal is to leave people charged, to provide them with tools to better deal with the opportunities and challenges they face each day, and to provide a different viewpoint, a more positive perspective on their lives. The feedback I receive is almost always very positive, with one exception.

Many people who have attended my presentations inevitably send an e-mail or call a few months later and explain how they departed the presentation with renewed energy and a rekindled desire to excel. When they left, they had a full tank and were ready to roll on both a professional and personal level. But then, the very issues that drained their tanks in the first place had done so again. They felt they were right back where they started.

Just like the gas tank in your vehicle, eventually the level will run low in your personal emotional fuel tank and it would be a good idea to be near a gas station or convenience store when that happens. Unfortunately, when it comes to enthusiasm for our jobs and our lives, some of us don't live near refueling stations and we definitely don't work near them. We just don't have the opportunity to pull-in for an "enthusiasm re-fill" when our personal "low fuel" light comes on.

To address this need identified by my audiences I began to write and distribute a weekly leadership article for the attendees of my presentations, using short essays to support one of the points we covered in our time together. I still send an original *Catch Fire* by email each week.

The feedback has been tremendous and the distribution list has grown. I very often receive a call or e-mail from someone wanting to know if it is okay to forward *Catch Fire* to employees, colleagues, friends...even their bosses. My answer is always the same. "Absolutely."

It is not unusual to receive an e-mail from a person who never even attended one of my sessions describing how these weekly emails have literally changed their lives. While that seems a little dramatic, I have come to learn that people do look forward to *Catch Fire* and many people count on these short articles for support, for that "emotional re-fill," each of us need from time to time.

After writing dozens of these, I have come to view a few of them as my personal favorites, the ones that hold special meaning for me. And with input from many readers, I have also been able to clearly determine which articles have really hit the mark in helping people reignite the leadership flame that burns within.

This book represents some of the best of my work to date. Its short, digestible chapters can be read quickly and immediately implemented in your daily life. It is intended to be that "re-fueling" stop on the days when obstacles seem to outnumber opportunities and the desire for a positive attitude is overcome by the reality of the day.

This book is intended to help managers become leaders and assist people who want to stay positive about their jobs and their lives. I urge you to take the information you find here and live it. Simply reading or talking about it will have limited effect. Long-term impact comes only when you actively use what you learn.

Specific elements are necessary to initiate and sustain a fire. Oxygen, heat and fuel must be present for combustion to take place. I'm excited to share with you the key elements that I believe are necessary for successful leadership. I hope you accept the challenge to burn brightly and become a blue flame that lights the way for your people.

Put Both Feet in the Fire

LEADERSHIP DEFINED

IF YOUR ACTIONS INSPIRE OTHERS
TO DREAM MORE, LEARN MORE,
DO MORE AND BECOME MORE,
YOU ARE A LEADER.

JOHN QUINCY ADAMS

Making the Decision
To Be Different

LEADERSHIP IS NOT AN ASSIGNMENT. Leadership is a decision. The truth is your job title doesn't make you a leader. Neither does your education. In fact, leadership cannot be bestowed upon you. The only way leadership occurs in a lasting and meaningful way is when you make a decision to make a difference. But what does it really mean to make a difference? In our everyday lives, how do we know we are thinking and acting like leaders?

There probably is no sure-fire leadership test. However, there are a few traits that are common in people who have made the decision to be leaders.

LEADERS DON'T WAIT.
Leaders understand they can't wait for those around them or their organizations to change. When the time for action comes, leaders act first and act with confidence. It is so easy to blame others for lack of progress. True leaders don't use that excuse and initiate change themselves.

LEADERS CHANGE FROM WITHIN.
Leaders recognize that change starts at home. As individuals and as organizations, we have to grow change from the inside. Leaders don't tell others how to do better. They provide a vision and model the way. Leaders have an uncommon ability and willingness to see past today's problems and recognize the potential of the future and then initiate a course of action that provides hope for all those involved.

LEADERS KNOW WHAT MATTERS.

Everyone can't win every time. However, leaders have the ability and, again, the willingness, to make sure there are no losers in a given situation. Leaders understand the importance of creating win-win outcomes and see the value in preserving dignity. Leaders know it doesn't matter who is right, only what is right.

LEADERS ARE POSITIVE AND OPTIMISTIC.

But not particularly in a rah-rah way. Leaders provide a refreshing and hopeful example for what is possible. No one wants to follow someone down a dirt road. Most people want to go to the mountaintop and they are going to follow people they believe will get them there. Leaders attract people with their attitude and their vision. It is not manufactured nor contrived. Leaders naturally attract and it is that attraction, however difficult it may be to identify, that helps define them as leaders.

LEADERSHIP IS A WAY OF LIFE.
YOU CAN'T TURN IT OFF
AT THE END OF THE DAY.

If you're not sure where you fall on the leadership continuum, measure yourself against these traits. Even if you don't have the formal title or the fancy office or the stock options, you could very well still be a leader. On the other hand, just because you have the formal title, the office and the compensation, it doesn't make you a leader.

Pure and simple, leaders make a difference. It may be at home or at the office or at church, whatever the situation, we all have the opportunity to lead. We have the opportunity to make a difference. And we don't have to wait until someone gives us permission.

First and foremost, leaders have to make the decision to lead. While the opportunity to lead may be the result of circumstances, the decision to seize that opportunity must be just that—a decision. Leadership doesn't happen by accident. People are not forced into a leadership role.

Leadership is a way of life. You can't turn it off at the end of the day. We are who we are 24 hours a day, seven days a week. Seriously ask yourself how you rank in the areas listed above. If you choose to become a better leader, focus on these things and your leadership skills will improve.

You don't have to wait for an invitation to impact those around you. There is no reason to feel frustrated and powerless in your situation. You don't always have to go with the flow. By choosing to become a leader, you can change your own situation and the situations of those around you.

The greatest changes in society have almost always been the result of actions initiated by a single person. At the time the action was initiated, it may not have seemed all that significant. Today is the day to initiate change in your life or your organization. Don't wait for permission. Don't wait for a promotion. Make a decision and make a difference. That is true leadership!

Leading versus Managing: What are You Doing?

A SENIOR EXECUTIVE ASKED me a very interesting question recently. He explained that, in his company, he is very hands-on and involved in day-to-day business activities, but he is also expected to be a leader. He wanted to know how much of what he is doing is managing and how much of it is leading—and, more importantly, how he could focus on doing more of the latter.

The good news is he understood there is a difference in the two. In the dictionary, managing is defined as being "in charge of something such as a store, department, or project and being responsible for its smooth running and for any personnel employed." It defines leadership as "the ability to guide, direct, or influence people."

In terms that I think relate more directly to our conversation, we can look at things slightly differently. For our purposes, you *manage* a process, and you *lead* people. So the answer to the executive's question actually has multiple angles:

In your job, you will need to lead and manage every day, sometimes simultaneously.

1) It is critical to understand the difference between leading and managing. People do not respond well to being managed, but they almost always enjoy being led.

2) You can manage all day and never lead. Therefore, just because you are a manager does not automatically make you a leader.

3) Managing almost always has a definable result (profit/loss, win/lose, etc.), while leading does not always produce such identifiable outcomes.

4) Managing is more of a short-term proposition, while leading is ongoing.

5) Managing takes a different set of skills than those required for leading.

6) Managing is easier than leading. That's why we have more managers in this world than we have leaders. That's why leaders stand out. No one ever had a tombstone that says, "He was a great manager." However, many tombstones out there say, "He was a great leader."

7) Managing sometimes requires brute force. Leading never does.

The key word in the definition of leadership is "influence." I believe leadership is what happens when you leave a room. What kind of "influence" have you left behind that makes your people want to do what needs to get done?

I BELIEVE LEADERSHIP IS WHAT HAPPENS
WHEN YOU LEAVE A ROOM.

And let's face it: in today's hectic times, we can only get so much done ourselves in a single workday. We physically run out of time to do it all ourselves. We have to be able to influence others to accomplish that which needs to be done, and this is where leadership comes into play. Leaders envision the desired outcome and then help everyone achieve that outcome. Leaders pave the road. Managers often find themselves dealing with the people who get off the road.

I think the most profound difference in managing and leading lies in what kind of "mental aftertaste" we have at the end of the day. Managers have spent most of the day trying to keep the train on the tracks and correct what has gone wrong. On the other hand, leaders have spent the day helping everyone understand why the train needs to keep moving and where it is going. It is the difference in the forward-looking perspective of a leader versus the today-and-backward perspective of a manager.

Don't get me wrong. We have to be realists and deal with problems as they occur. Even the person at the top can't be a leader every minute. Managing has to occur at all levels of an organization. What I am saying is that if you read the descriptions above and find you are managing much more than you are leading, then you have the equation reversed. If you spend more time leading, you will have to spend less time managing.

When your people have a very good idea of where they need to go, they are much better equipped to get there by themselves…without being managed. Balance is the key to any professional's life. If you spend all your time putting out fires, you'll never have any time to prevent future ones.

It is very useful to schedule at least a few minutes every day to be forward-thinking. Let go of what is happening at that minute, and think about what can be done to move forward and reach the desired outcome. Then act on your conclusion and communicate it to your people. That is leadership. If *you* don't do it in your company, it may just not get done. Your company has managers; what it needs is leaders.

Leading versus Managing: What are You Doing? (Part 2)

TODAY'S WORKFORCE IS MORE DIVERSE THAN EVER BEFORE. The "my-way-or-the-highway" style of management just doesn't cut it anymore. And while the hard-nosed approach doesn't work in the current business environment, simply allowing employees to march to their own beat is not the answer either. In fact, the answer lies somewhere in between, and it really brings us to the very definition of what leadership involves.

Your people have to make decisions every day without you or any other "boss" around. You simply cannot stand over them and, in real-time, dictate each decision to make sure they are doing what they are supposed to do. In fact, if your success is based on your ability to directly manage your people, you are behind the curve…possibly fatally behind the curve.

THE TRUTH IS, YOU MANAGE A PROCESS,
WHILE YOU LEAD PEOPLE.

We have discussed the definition of "leadership." That description becomes most useful when compared to "management." The truth is, you *manage* a process, while you *lead* people. People do not take well to being "managed," especially when management takes the form of telling people what they are doing wrong or need to do differently. "Leadership is not something you do *to* people" leadership expert Ken Blanchard says in his book *The Heart of a Leader*. "It is something you do *with* them." In fact, leadership is the opposite of trying to control them.

Leaders determine and communicate the preferred outcome and then help their people achieve that preferred outcome. They lay out the goals and objectives, and then they provide the tools, the encouragement, and the values the workforce needs to achieve the goals. Leaders don't play the blame game. Leaders focus on the future and, while learning from the past, let go of it and focus like a laser on what lies ahead. What do we want to be? Where do we want to go? That is leadership focus.

Each of us, on a regular basis, should step back from the day-to-day grind and ask ourselves if we are managing or leading. Are we doing things *to* our people or *with* them? Are we *helping* them focus on where we want to go or *making* them focus on where we have been? The truth is, in this world where we spend a great deal of time putting out fires, trying to keep customers and employees happy, and generally trying to deal with each crisis as it arises, it is very easy to become more of a manager than a leader.

But probably the greatest trait of leaders, and the one that results in real integrity, is the leaders' ensuring that their actions are consistent with their words. Leaders simply live their lives as the people they want their employees to be. They don't tell people to be at work on time and then show up an hour after everyone else. Leaders don't talk about the importance of treating others well and then behave disrespectfully. Leaders talk the talk *and* walk the walk. Leadership doesn't start at the top; it starts with every member of an organization every day on every issue.

You simply cannot take a timeout from being a leader. That one time you blow up or say something hurtful or admonish someone in public will show your people that you don't live up to your own expectations of them. Your people are always watching you to decide how they should act—even when you don't realize it. Unfortunately, leaders are often defined by the exceptions to their lives and not the rule.

So the next time you feel stressed or maybe even frustrated by what is going on in your company or your department, step back and look at yourself. Have you become a manager instead of a leader? Are you sending the wrong messages to your people? Have you become exactly what you don't want them to be? Are you doing your job, as a leader, to model the way for your employees?

Being a leader is not easy. Whether you like it or not, you are almost always in the spotlight, and you are judged by a higher standard. You are expected to perform when others don't. In fact, your very existence often revolves around making sure the ship is sailing in the right direction, even when it appears all hope is lost, and the ship is taking on water.

Leaders don't direct; they provide direction. Leaders don't "fix" things; they provide tools so their people can "fix" the problems on their own. Leaders provide an example of what and how their people should be.

We all have times when we need to step back and evaluate ourselves, our strategy, and our motives. If your goal is to lay out the desired outcome and to help every employee arrive in the same place, then you truly are leading. If your goal is something different, you may be falling short of your role as a leader and creating more problems than you are solving.

The Power of Passion

NOW THAT WE HAVE CLEARLY defined the differences between managing and leading, I would like to talk about that in the context of passion.

To do so, we have to first get our hands around the definition of "passion." Let's begin by making sure we don't confuse passion with emotion. Passion expands and even sharpens our horizons, often providing us with a keen sense of awareness because of our increased interest and sensitivity. Conversely, emotion often clouds our viewpoint. It can cause us to narrow our perspective, while passion can broaden that same perspective.

Now let's look at the difference in the passion of a manager versus the passion of a leader. To do so, we can go back to one of the basic differences in managing and leading. Remember, we "manage" a process; we "lead" people. In that context, managers have passion for what they do. Leaders may as well. But great leaders also have a passion for the people around them. They understand that they are limited in what they can do personally but unlimited in what they can accomplish through those around them.

Do you have as much passion for helping your people succeed as you do for succeeding personally? Is your top priority to reach a personal goal or to help your people reach theirs? Is your passion to complete a task or to provide others the tools they need so they can complete the task? Are you willing to give and even excited about your people receiving the credit for what goes right in your company?

The effect of passion is almost always profound, because it comes from our deepest motivations. People with passion don't just enjoy the destination, they enjoy the journey. People with passion don't sit around all day waiting for five or six o'clock to come around so they can resume living their lives. They know that work is part of their lives and something to embrace and enjoy, not something to "get over with."

Think about the passion and enthusiasm that children have for much of what they do. They are often not developed enough to know when to give up. They do an activity because they want to. They don't particularly care about being judged on their performance, although they certainly seem to enjoy encouragement. What if we could carry the passion of our childhood into our adult lives? What if we do what we do because we love it and embrace the activity, not just do it because it's our job?

WHAT IF WE COULD CARRY
THE PASSION OF OUR CHILDHOOD
INTO OUR ADULT LIVES?

I am often saddened by those people who don't feel that they have accomplished much in life. They go through each day hoping for something better around the next curve and simply never enjoy the scenery around them. What a passionless way to live life.

In our business careers, we are faced with challenges every day. Some are new, and some surface regularly. If we are waiting to be happy when we solve all our problems, we will be waiting a long, long time.

One of the ways we can enjoy our life and our work more is through the people around us. We may not have passion for the challenges we face each day, but we can have passion for the process of working through them. We can have passion for helping our people work through them. And we can have passion for seeing our people succeed.

The next time you find yourself feeling down and wishing five o'clock would come around, resist the temptation. Don't fall into the manager's trap. Understand that your role is to have passion...passion for the people around you, passion for their success, and passion for the journey, not just the destination.

Leaders have an additional burden. But that burden doesn't have to be negative. When you have passion for leadership, it is not a problem. It's an opportunity. When others wish people would leave them alone, leaders know that their true power, their true effectiveness comes through those very people around them.

Have passion for your people, and the rest will take care of itself. Be a leader today and every day—a leader with passion!

The Five Greatest Challenges of a Leader

MANY OF THE PEOPLE who come through my leadership programs are younger leaders who are working their way up the ladder and, in many cases, getting their first taste of the responsibility that comes with the title of being "boss." Others have already completed the trek up the chain of command and know too well the challenges and opportunities that come with being the ultimate decision-maker.

Regardless of which category you fall into, from time to time you may be tempted to lose sight of what is important. We all are subject to the temptations that can befall any leader, regardless of age or experience, in any business. Following are what I believe to be the five greatest temptations of a leader. By understanding that these pitfalls may lie in our path, we are better able to avoid them.

BEING MORE FOCUSED ON ACTIVITY THAN RESULTS.

We want our people to be busy, and that is all well and good. However, what we should really want is results. When our focus becomes more on making sure our people are "doing something," we lose sight of the need to make sure they are doing the "right" things that produce results. Make sure compensation and incentives reward results and not just activities. Busy people can go broke; effective people usually don't.

WORRYING ABOUT AND MANAGING THE WRONG THINGS.

What is important in your organization? You have to know the answer to this question to know what to measure and manage. What you manage should be directly in line with your objectives and goals. From a business perspective, if what you are paying attention to does not fall in line with the desired results, then everyone's time can be wasted. From a personal prospective, you can drive yourself nuts by getting all worked up over issues that, at the end of the day, just don't matter.

PEOPLE DECIDE HOW TO TREAT
FELLOW EMPLOYEES AND CUSTOMERS
BY WATCHING YOU.

NOT REMEMBERING THAT PEOPLE ARE WATCHING EVERY MOVE YOU MAKE.

The emotional wake you leave behind as a leader is significant. People decide how to treat fellow employees and customers by watching you. Every decision you make, regardless of whether that decision is right, wrong, or somewhere in between, has consequences. Understanding this premise can help you in your decision-making process and help you have a greater passion for more thoughtful decision making and less knee-jerk emotional reaction.

BEING SO WRAPPED UP IN BEING RIGHT THAT YOU ARE BLINDED TO THE TRUTH.

Younger leaders are especially susceptible to this temptation. When you are working your way up the corporate ladder, it is often difficult to accept outside input or criticism and to admit mistakes. The truth is that the most enlightened leaders have the confidence to be open-minded about their own limitations. The sooner leaders understand they don't have all the answers, the sooner they will understand the need to be surrounded by great people. Don't be afraid to hire people who could take your job; don't be afraid to accept input. You don't have to follow the input, but you should at least be open to hearing it.

FAILING TO PROVIDE WHAT YOUR PEOPLE NEED.

The role of a leader is to have and communicate a vision of the preferred outcome and then to provide the people in the organization the tools to achieve that preferred outcome. The first without the second almost completely eliminates anyone's opportunity for success. As legendary pro golfer Lee Trevino once said, "99 percent of the putts that don't get to the hole have no chance of going in." Likewise, we can encourage our people all we want to, but if we don't give them the tools they need to succeed, they won't. That's not their fault. It becomes the fault of the leader.

Unfortunately, experience does not insulate a leader from the temptations above. In fact, all of us will face these issues more than once in our professional and personal lives. However, each time we deal with them, we should be better able to recognize the symptoms when they reappear. This self-awareness is like a flu shot of sorts. By dealing with these temptations and having them in our system, we are better able to resist them the next time.

Great leaders know themselves very well. By understanding our potential weaknesses and challenges, we are better able to deal with them.

Building an Organization from the Ground Up

A FEW BASIC RULES APPLY to business organizations and those who work in them. When we understand these and apply them to our organizations, we significantly improve our opportunities to excel both as leaders and as business operations.

COMPANIES DO WHAT THE BOSS DOES.

Obviously, companies can't do *anything*. But the people that make up the companies can. And these people take their cues from the boss in many ways. How the boss acts, how the boss talks, how the boss dresses—all these things are direct messages, from the top, on how to conduct business. We have talked about the emotional wake left by the boss's decisions, but the behavioral wake that each of us leaves should never be underestimated. Why should we expect our people to act any differently than we do? We shouldn't.

WEAK MANAGERS HIRE WEAK PEOPLE TO WORK FOR THEM.

Managers who lack confidence will very often surround themselves with people who lack confidence. Why? Because they don't want to hire anyone who could take their jobs. The truth is, great managers surround themselves with great people. In fact, they often intentionally hire people who could take their jobs. Why? Because they are not threatened. When a department is not meeting expectations, we often ask the department head what is wrong. In fact, the department head can very well be the problem and, if he is, he may very well have a department full of problems if he was responsible for hiring. By understanding that mediocrity attracts more mediocrity, we can save ourselves a great deal of heartache and wasted effort by cutting off a dead tree at its roots instead of trying to save it one branch at a time.

HIRE THE BEST, WEED OUT THE REST.

For a variety of reasons, we often justify holding on to employees that don't meet expectations. Sometimes we do it in the name of loyalty. Sometimes we don't have a better alternative. Other times, it is just easier not to make a change. The truth is, we are only as strong as our weakest employee. The top priority of any company, ahead of almost anything else, should be to hire the best people. We often kid ourselves into thinking we can't afford the best. In actuality, we can't afford not to hire the best. Part of any company's strategic process each year should be to identify the weak links in the personnel chain and to work to replace them. The personnel issues will not correct themselves, and the longer they are allowed to fester, the worse it will be for the organization.

YOU CAN'T OVER-COMMUNICATE WHAT IS IMPORTANT.

Many of the problems we have in business are due to a lack of communication. It is not possible to talk too much about expectations, goals, and objectives. Whatever you have done, as a leader, to communicate expectations—do more. Your people have to know what is expected if they are to achieve it. Almost all great leaders are great communicators; their people understand what is expected and often work tirelessly to achieve it. When we make communication a top priority, we truly are putting our efforts where they are most needed.

WHATEVER YOU HAVE DONE
TO COMMUNICATE EXPECTATIONS—
DO MORE.

The world is full of truisms: the sky is blue on a clear day. Flowers are a welcome sight in the springtime. Fire burns. Money can't buy you happiness, but it can provide a nice down-payment. We could go on and on.

In applying the four business truisms listed above, we can greatly improve our opportunities for success in business and as leaders. We can also provide a much more positive environment in which our people can succeed. And when our people succeed, we succeed.

Using the Power of
Your Own Words

NEARLY FIFTEEN YEARS AGO, I accidentally wound up in a presentation by a motivational speaker. I was not even supposed to be there, but that presentation changed my life. The speaker had no idea I was there, but still, the words the speaker delivered that day opened my eyes and changed my attitude forever. He didn't know it at the time, and neither did I.

The speaker's name was Dewitt Jones. At that time, he was a photographer for *National Geographic*. He traveled the world taking the kind of photographs we all grew up seeing in that magazine. Later, he had parlayed that job into a career as a motivational speaker. In his talks, he accentuated his message with a slide presentation of the many incredible photos he had taken around the globe.

THE WORDS HE DELIVERED THAT DAY
OPENED MY EYES AND CHANGED MY
ATTITUDE FOREVER.

At that time in my life, I was very selfish, and I absolutely was paying attention to the wrong things. My priorities were not really *wrong*, it was more that I didn't *have* priorities. Going into that room that day, I was not really interested in anything Dewitt said, or anything any motivational speaker had to say, for that matter. But somehow, the words he spoke, together with the images he shared, convinced me of how fortunate I was at that time to be living in this great country, working at a great job for great people in a great industry. It wasn't some religious experience in which I wanted to go down to the front of the room and declare a new start. The presentation's impact was much more subtle in the beginning, yet powerful in the long run. I can't explain it, and it probably wouldn't make sense if I did. You had to be in my head to get it.

I have seen Dewitt several times since then. The second time I saw him was three years after I first heard his presentation. By then, I knew what he had meant in my life, and I shared my feelings with him. He was touched, and a few days later I received a gift from him in the mail. On a plastic toy camera (remember, he was a photographer) he had written, "Keep the vision." Of course, he signed the gift, and today—twelve years later—that toy camera sits in a prominent place in my office.

Dewitt Jones didn't wake up that morning intending to change my life. And I certainly didn't get up planning to have my life changed. As I said earlier, it was literally an accident I was even in the room; I was supposed to be somewhere else. However, the experience happened, and I'll never forget it.

As leaders, our words can be just as powerful as Dewitt's were to me, either in a positive or a negative way. I often talk about the "emotional wake" of our words and actions. Sometimes we don't even realize the impact of what we say. But when we are truly thinking as leaders, we take every opportunity we can to use the positive power of our words to help our people succeed.

I would never ask you to manipulate the people around you. However, I would absolutely encourage you to understand the importance of what you say and to be as positive and supportive as possible with your employees. In today's challenging business environment, and even at home, we hear plenty of negatives. Your role as a leader should be to continually provide encouragement—encouragement of the heart as well as the brain—to those around you.

I challenge you to be positive every opportunity you get. When others are down, you stay up. When others are condescending, you be encouraging. When others can't get the picture, you paint it for them in vivid colors. Sure, it's a challenge, and sometimes it may even seem like a burden. But remember, leadership is a choice, not an assignment. You don't get to be a leader just when it is convenient. You never know when your words, your encouragement, might just change someone's life.

Start today. This may just be the day when what you say helps people overcome a challenge; you could help them keep going when they think quitting might be an easier option. You don't have to be a motivational speaker to accomplish this. As a leader, your words mean a great deal, and if you are in touch with your role in your business, you are well aware of that. Get out of your office, and spend time with your people; they need you and may not even know it.

I needed Dewitt Jones that day and didn't even know it. He changed my life nearly fifteen years ago. As a leader, you could have the opportunity to do the same today or tomorrow or the next day for someone in your life or business, even though you may not even know when it is happening. Your words mean a great deal, so be positive. Choose your words wisely. You never know when you and your words will make the difference in someone else's life.

Having a Vision is More Than a Paranormal Experience

ONE OF THE KEY ATTRIBUTES OF A LEADER IS THE ABILITY, and willingness, to focus on the preferred outcome. Where do we want to go? What do we want to be when we get there? Who will be with us when we arrive? The answers to all these questions lead us to the *vision* that we must provide our people. In fact, great leaders are almost always known for their vision.

If we don't know where we are going, how are we going to know when we get there? More importantly, if we don't have a vision, and don't share it with our people, how can they know when they (we) are achieving success? The answer is that our people are internally motivated to reach a goal when they have a clear vision of that goal. For them to have a clear vision, we, as leaders, must have a clear vision—and share it. How clear is your vision these days?

We often need to clean our glasses or even the windshield in our car to bring our vision into sharper focus, and the same thing is true of our vision as leaders. The daily challenges we all face can blur our vision from time to time. Throw in the distractions that often accompany setbacks in the form of missed deadlines, personnel problems, and challenging customers—and we can downright lose our vision completely.

How can we, as leaders who have a responsibility to maintain and provide a meaningful vision for our people, clean our own glasses on a periodic basis and ensure that we have not lost sight of where we are headed? The answer, just as in many other cases, requires self-discipline and a self-awareness that comes with recognizing the need to refocus from time to time.

Following are a few simple steps to help continually renew our ability and willingness to first maintain the vision we need as leaders and then to share that vision with those around us.

WE SHOULD TRY TO BLOCK OUT
AT LEAST ONE HOUR PER DAY OR HALF
A DAY EACH WEEK TO WORK ON
NOTHING BUT LONG-TERM ISSUES.

KEEP FOCUSED DOWNRANGE.

We often get so fixated on the trees, we lose sight of the forest. While leaders certainly need to pay attention to detail, we must maintain our long-term visual acuity. Part of that self-awareness I discussed earlier is knowing when we have gotten too caught up in the small things. While leaders are responsible for vision, we must also have the commitment to let the people we have hired do their jobs. We must battle the tendency to get too caught up in the small things, to micro-manage. Instead, we should try to block out at least one hour per day or half a day each week to work on nothing but long-term issues. We should use this time to free our mind of today's problems and focus on tomorrow's solutions.

HELP MAINTAIN THE PROPER FOCUS.

Great leaders help their people focus on the right things. Part of our ability to maintain our vision is our willingness to focus on what we want more of as opposed to focusing on what we want to eliminate. It is so easy to spend a great deal of time finding out what is "wrong" with our company or a particular situation. While there certainly is value in determining what is wrong, we can get caught up in looking for someone or something to blame and waste valuable effort and focus by failing to apply our energies to the solution. When you make the commitment to be forward-focused and solution-oriented, you will enhance your vision. After all, if the good Lord had meant for us to look backwards, he would have put eyes in the back of our heads (my grandmother would be proud...).

ALLOW TIME FOR PEOPLE TO "GET" IT.

While leadership has the responsibility for vision, the greater responsibility lies in sharing and communicating that vision. Communication, by definition, is a two-way process. Simply printing cards or posters with a vision statement is not communication. Leaders don't tell—leaders share. We can't lead by edict. For our people to buy into our vision, they have to share in it. Simply telling our people where we are going is not enough; we have to show them. This takes time—on both ends. Allow time to share your vision and time for your people to get it. Conduct a vision meeting at least once per month or once per quarter, a meeting in which you truly "share" your vision and allow your people the opportunity to absorb and understand it.

I have said many times that we can't know if we are winning the race if we have no idea where the finish line is located. And sure, as soon as we finish one race, another one starts. We may even be running more than one race at a time.

You owe it to yourself and your people to constantly define the finish line you should be aiming for and to provide the encouragement to get there. Vision is what gives people hope. Vision is what gives people direction. Vision is what sets a leader apart from a manager.

When you make the commitment to allow yourself the time and opportunity to identify a clear vision of the future, you are making a commitment to your business, your people, and yourself. When you follow that with a determination to share the vision, you are making a commitment to success.

The Boiling Point

I READ A GREAT SHORT ARTICLE RECENTLY about the power of one degree. It asks us to consider what happens to water when it reaches 211 degrees. Very little, actually. It is hot, and we might see some small bubbles begin to rise to the surface, but not much more. If the water remains at that temperature, nothing else happens.

However, add one degree of heat to that pot, and stand back. The power of that last degree, less than one-half of one percent, turns hot water into a churning power that can light a city or propel a locomotive. The first 211 degrees are important but mean little without that last degree.

As leaders, how do we coax that last degree, and beyond, from our people? How do we help them understand that performing to a certain level does us very little good if we can't provide that last push to meet our customers' demands? The first ninety yards of a hundred-yard dash are important. But you can have a two-second lead after ninety yards and still not win if you don't run that last ten yards. Companies get to 211 degrees every day. It is those who reach the boiling point that understand the importance of that last one-half of one percent of effort, which will result in excelling in today's competitive business environment. To get there you must do the following:

MAKE EXPECTATIONS CLEAR.

As we have discussed before, our people can't win the race if they don't know where the finish line is. Those we lead have a much better opportunity to excel if they know what is expected of them, if they know when it is time to reach back for that extra effort, when it is time to do what it takes to raise the temperature that one last degree. Be clear of what "success" means in your company, and outline clear and specific goals and objectives.

BE VISIBLE IN CRUCIAL TIMES.

As leaders, we have to be in the pot when the water begins to boil. When we most need our employees to perform at the highest level, we need to be standing beside them, encouraging them, and providing them with the tools they need to meet and exceed our expectations. In stressful times, people need to see their leaders.

PREPARE FOR WAR DURING PEACE.

Legendary college football coach Bear Bryant was once asked how important it is to make an inspirational speech to his players on game day. His answer speaks to his great success. He said, "These guys sweat and bleed every day practicing for Saturday. Their mamas and daddies are in that stadium to see them along with 70,000 other folks. We've run every play hundreds, if not thousands, of times. If we're not ready when we get to that stadium on Saturday, there's nothing I'm going to say that's going to get them ready." The best time to prepare for war is during peace. Provide your people with daily inspiration and the tools they need, and, when the time comes, they will perform.

PROVIDE YOUR PEOPLE WITH
DAILY INSPIRATION AND THE TOOLS
THEY NEED, AND, WHEN THE TIME
COMES, THEY WILL PERFORM.

HIRE THOROUGHBREDS AND LET THEM RUN.

Our people are good at what they do; that's why we hired them. Sometimes, despite our best efforts as leaders, we limit their capabilities by not always letting them do what we hired them to do. We need to be sure we don't get in the way of our employees' potential. Key times, when we are seeking those last few degrees, are when it is most important to let the system work and to let our horses run.

Leadership matters most when it is needed most. The key for each of us is to understand our role in the process. The first 211 degrees are important, but that last degree gets the pot boiling. Make sure you are leading your people when they most need to be led, and make sure you have a plan and a mechanism to generate that last bit of heat when it is required.

Our customers require a great deal of us. Our people are the ones who can and will deliver it, so make sure they are ready when the time comes. Your role as a leader is crucial, and now is the time to gear up for the key situations. You never know when that last degree will be needed.

How You Start Has a Lot to Do with How You Finish

HOW DO YOU START YOUR WORKDAY? One of my favorite singer/songwriters of all time is a Texas music legend by the name of Gary P. Nunn. With his musical roots planted alongside such greats as Willie Nelson and Waylon Jennings, Gary P. is known for crooning classic lyrics, including the words from one of his hit recordings of a song by Nelson, "The last thing I needed the first thing this morning is to have you walk out on me." While those words were written with love in mind, they can and often do apply to our workday as well.

Very often, the first thing that happens to you in the morning is the last thing you need. You may not have even gotten to your office before the bad news starts. Maybe you walked in the door already behind the eight ball because of car trouble, heavy traffic, or a problem at home. Even if you manage to get to work in one mental piece, bad news can come early and often and turn a good day into one of those "I wish I had never gotten out of bed" kind of mornings.

In a leadership position, you send signals to your people each and every day. Very few of these signals are neutral; they are almost always either positive or negative. Your employees observe these signals—your behavior—to decide how they should act themselves. Sometimes this process is conscious, and sometimes it is more a matter of attitudinal osmosis. Either way, the example you set early in the day can have a profound impact on your people and the way they act throughout the remainder of the workday.

THE EXAMPLE YOU SET EARLY IN THE
DAY CAN HAVE A PROFOUND IMPACT
ON YOUR PEOPLE AND THE WAY
THEY ACT THROUGHOUT THE
REMAINDER OF THE WORKDAY.

So, how do you make sure that you start the day on the right foot and thereby start your organization on the right foot? Here are a few keys:

UNDERSTAND YOUR ROLE.

It is important to understand that problems—no matter what time of the day they occur—are not necessarily problems. In fact, without problems, most of us would be out of a job. You can spend the rest of your life hoping problems will go away, but doing so will waste a lot of energy. Your role is to effectively deal with problems that occur. You can begin the process of insuring you begin the day well by understanding that problems and issues are the job and that effectively dealing with them is an opportunity and not an obstacle. Your attitude toward the issues you face will significantly impact how well you deal with them, so if you begin the day looking for challenges, you will deal with them better.

THE EARLY BIRD.

One way to at least get a leg up on your challenges each day is to start early. Often, if you can arrive early and get your day in order before the phone begins ringing and trouble comes knocking, you are much better able to deal with what comes your way. When you haven't even had time to drink that first cup of coffee or to open your e-mail, you often resent the issues that come your way and don't face them with the right attitude. That is not fair to you or to whoever is talking on the other end of the line or walking into your office. Start the day early and be better prepared for what will eventually happen.

MAKE A DECISION.

The only thing you can control on a daily basis is your attitude. It may sound trite, but the best way to ensure that you will have a great day is to make the decision to have a great day. Decide to walk into your office each day with a positive attitude. When you sense yourself slipping, catch yourself. Leave yourself reminders that people are watching you and that you should keep a positive attitude. Don't fall into the negative trap that can cost you and your organization efficiency, customers, and hard dollars. You cannot realistically expect your people to be positive if you are not. They will take signals from you; it's up to you to make sure they are the right signals.

Life and work can be difficult enough on their own; you don't need to make things worse by falling victim to the downs that inevitably accompany the ups. Being a leader requires maintaining a higher standard, even in the face of obstacles and challenges. By understanding the importance of beginning the day on a positive note, you can proactively control your own actions and, ultimately, the actions of others.

The way you begin the day will have an impact on the rest of the day. Deciding to start on the right foot will make a difference for you and your organization. Enlightened leaders understand the emotional wake they leave throughout the day. Make sure the wake you're leaving behind is a positive one.

So the next time the last thing you need happens first thing in the morning, make the decision to deal with it effectively and stay positive. Your people are depending on it.

Begin Each New Year with the Right Plan...and the Right Tools

WHILE THE HOLIDAY SEASON CAN BE VERY ENJOYABLE, it can also be hectic. Shopping for gifts, attending holiday parties, visiting relatives, and coping with key staffers out on vacation are just some of the issues that can make December a challenge.

On the other hand, the final weeks of the year can also be a time of inspiration, planning, and great optimism. In fact, many of us use the downtime over the holidays, when the rest of the world seems to shut down, to clear our desks and minds in order to prepare for a fresh new year.

As is the case with many New Year's resolutions, our hopes and even our plans don't always play out as we had anticipated. What seemed like a great idea on the quiet day before Christmas never quite reaches its full potential in the months that follow. Why is this? Part of the problem is that we don't always provide the tools, the direction, and the follow-through needed to see an idea from concept to completion.

So if you have grand ideas for how things will be different for your company in the year ahead, make sure you keep the following hints in mind to help ensure a successful start to each year.

KNOW WHAT YOU WANT.

People will perform to the level at which they are expected to perform. They can only meet expectations if you make clear what you want or need. In order to convey your expectations, you first have to clearly know what you want.

Saying you want your company to be "more profitable" is not clear. What does "more profitable" mean? You have to accurately know the desired outcome before you and/or your people can achieve it.

COMMUNICATE YOUR VISION.

Once you have defined what you need, communicate it, communicate it, and communicate it some more. One of the biggest problems we have as leaders is assuming that our people understand what we mean; they often don't. If we can't put into a few, simple words what we are after, then we don't have a clear understanding ourselves (see the item above). Be as clear with your communication as you are with the vision in your head.

BE COMMITTED.

Your people will watch how you act and react to decide how they will act and react. You have to be committed to your vision, your idea. If you are not, your people will see it in you and will act on that lack of commitment. Leaders lead by example. Rest assured, when you give up on an idea or an objective, your people will, as well. You can't fool them for very long. And, by the way, when you do decide that something is not going to work, pull the plug. People have a limited amount of focus, and if you require them to use it on an idea you have abandoned, you are wasting their energy.

REST ASSURED, WHEN YOU GIVE UP
ON AN IDEA OR AN OBJECTIVE, YOUR
PEOPLE WILL AS WELL. YOU CAN'T
FOOL THEM FOR VERY LONG.

PROVIDE THE TOOLS AND RESOURCES.

Lasting change requires change at every level, and that often means a change in resources. Just asking your people to change their behavior without providing the tools and resources to do so can be a waste of time. Under the "be committed" banner, you must be willing to do what it takes to make something work, even if that means allocating additional assets or giving up some of the sacred cows that we all hold on to.

Most of us are at a point in our professional lives where our success depends on others. If we have grand plans for the new year for our company, it will take the active participation of all those around us to make the grand plans become real, measurable, and manageable objectives. If we leaders follow the tips above, we can fulfill our roles and truly lead change as opposed to demanding it. And that, my friends, is how you start off the year on the right foot!

The Importance of
Letting Go of Yesterday

FORMER PRESIDENT BILL CLINTON was tagged by some "The Teflon President" because of the inability of many of his critics to make negative charges against him stick. He seemed to be able to let bad news simply slip right off him. Despite all the criticism of his conduct and his policies, he always seemed to wear a smile in public.

Whether or not you agree with his behavior or his politics, President Clinton exhibited a trait that many great leaders share. In fact, it is very difficult, if not impossible, for a leader to excel without the ability to "get over it," so to speak.

How good are you at letting go of yesterday's bad news? How effective are you at not letting last week's problems impact today's decisions? How willing are you to not hold last month's mistakes against your people this month?

Great leaders are very good at freeing themselves, and their employees, from the baggage of the past. They understand that being forward-focused is a healthy perspective. Most importantly, great leaders know the power of having a clear vision and a positive mindset when tackling today's complex issues.

Unfortunately, many of us are faced with a long list of challenges, many coming rapid fire in a typical day. It is very difficult to not carry the emotion of one situation into the next. The first key is to understand why it is very important to avoid this potentially damaging behavior.

First, it is simply not fair to take out our frustrations on one employee for the actions, or lack thereof, of another. Second, when our minds are clouded by negative emotion, it often blocks the clear vision we need to make good decisions. Finally, when we are not able to separate and compartmentalize our challenges, we can quickly come to the conclusion, and resulting frustration, that our problems are too big to overcome.

So, how do we effectively manage our emotions and leave yesterday's problems out of today's business?

CLEAR YOUR EMOTIONAL SLATE.

The first key to managing carryover emotions is to realize they exist. Don't wait for someone near you to ask, "What's bothering you?" Before you take on a new challenge, in the form of a phone call or a face-to-face conversation, take a deep breath and clear your mind. You are the only one who can control your attitude. Clean your own slate, and enter a new challenge with a fresh perspective.

> CLEAN YOUR OWN SLATE,
> AND ENTER A NEW CHALLENGE
> WITH A FRESH PERSPECTIVE.

DON'T PROCRASTINATE.

Part of the reason we carry our emotions with us longer than we should is because we don't make the decisions we know we need to make. And the longer we go without making them, the more we know we are not meeting our own expectations. Failure to act in key situations does more to cripple us as leaders than anything else we can do. Don't let the failure to act on previous issues impact your ability to deal with future ones.

RESIST THE TEMPTATION TO TRANSFER STRESS.

It is not unusual for many of us to want to share our misery with others. I've heard people say, "I'm not the only one that is going to have to deal with this. Welcome to my world!" The only thing worse than not positively addressing your own issues is to drag other people into them as well. There is nothing to be gained by "sharing your misery," simply for the sake of making sure someone else knows what a bad day you're having. Enlightened leaders share their challenges, but they do it in a way that helps promote a solution. Get beyond what's wrong to what can be done to make it right.

President Clinton may or may not have been "The Teflon President." However, he overcame significant challenges, albeit some brought on himself, and possessed an uncanny ability to shake off bad news. As leaders, that is an ability that, used effectively, can help us stay focused on solutions and not be imprisoned by past challenges or failures.

Our people deserve our best at all times. They don't need to be hampered by our past, and they shouldn't have to endure the emotional baggage we carry from one situation to the next.

Handle every situation based on its own merits and challenges, and you'll find you have a clearer vision from which to lead. You may not be the "Teflon Leader," but you'll sure find it easier to deal with life's challenges one at a time.

Observing Our Own Best Practices

ONE OF THE MOST EFFECTIVE TOOLS you can use in business today is to benchmark against other companies and then use the collective best practices of those companies to improve your own operations. However, the greatest source of best practices is right under your own nose—literally.

To get where you are in business and in life, you must have done many things very well. While it is clearly valuable to look at what others do well and use your observations as a model, you can reap substantial value from reviewing your own actions to determine what you accomplished and what decisions were responsible for your success—and then doing more of the same thing!

We very often look back to learn from our mistakes. How about looking back to learn from our successes? Here's how we might accomplish this bit of behavioral replay:

CLEAR YOUR MIND.

This kind of thinking can't be done with the phone ringing and people coming in and out of your office. Pick a time and a location where you can think. A long airplane trip might be a good environment.

MAKE A LIST.

Literally, think back to the three best decisions or actions you can remember in your business or personal life. Write each of them on a separate, blank piece of paper.

RECREATE THE SCENE.

Take each action or decision separately. Recall under what circumstances you operated during that time. Take note of things like how much time you had to think through the issue, who you might have called on to provide counsel, or what information or book you read that inspired you. Try to recall anything of relevance to that situation.

RECREATE THE DECISION.

If at all possible, try to take your mind back to that time. What steps did you take to finally make the decision? How confident were you? The truth is, we are sometimes frozen out of making difficult decisions because we are not sure about what we are about to do. The truth is, we may often look back at previous good decisions, and remember that we were not at all confident when we pulled the trigger then, either.

PUT TODAY'S ISSUES IN CONTEXT.

Times change—but not as much as we think sometimes. We may now be leading more people or a bigger budget, but the underlying framework we use to make decisions probably hasn't changed. We are who we are, and while we may grow in our business knowledge and wisdom, it is likely that the basic foundation upon which we operate has not changed. However, sometimes who we are gets crowded out by the noise of our daily activities. I'm not trying to sound like your Zen master, but sometimes we need to shut out the noise and listen to what we know is right when we face difficult circumstances.

BELIEVE IN WHO YOU ARE.

When all is said and done, believe in yourself. You didn't get where you are making bad decisions. Counsel from those around you is always very important. However, the buck often stops with you. Being a leader is not easy. The decisions often are difficult and, more importantly, affect others in sometimes profound ways. A CEO once told one of his direct reports, "Ninety-five percent of the decisions you have to make could be made by any relatively informed college graduate. It's the other 5 percent I pay you for."

LEARNING FROM YOUR MISTAKES
IS FINE, BUT LEARNING FROM YOUR
SUCCESSES IS EVEN BETTER.

The next time you consider best practices, think of your own best practices, and use them again. Recall what you did right, and do more of it. Learning from your mistakes is fine, but learning from your successes is even better. You have accomplished great things to get where you are. Use that history to help with the future, and you will be a better leader.

The Decisions You Fail to Make Are the Ones That Can Break You

I BELIEVE THE DECISIONS THAT CAN MOST DAMAGE our careers are the ones we fail to make. Sure, we will all make decisions that turn out not to be the best choice given the facts at hand. Every now and then, we'll even make some real bonehead decisions. We all do it at some time in our life. But more often than not, the decisions we make will be the right ones, relatively speaking, and bring us the results we were after. It is those decisions we *don't* make that we should be most concerned about.

Many of us keep "to-do" lists. We feel very satisfied when, by the end of the day or the end of the week, we have worked our way through that list. But there may be one item that we have carried over for several days or weeks. We always find a way to justify not dealing with it; we just don't get it done for whatever reason.

Maybe the item involves having a talk with a long-time employee, even a relative, who is not performing up to standards. It could involve a problem customer. It could be as simple as a financial decision (not so simple sometimes) about whether to purchase something. Whatever the issue, we just can't (or won't) pull the trigger. It is these decisions that can, and often do, cause us the greatest amount of angst.

Procrastination is the greatest obstacle to leadership. Procrastination blocks our creative thinking by binding our thoughts. We use our energy up in avoiding the decision instead of processing the facts to make the decision. That's right: you can't just *not* make a decision. You have to make a conscious effort to not make a decision, and that uses up valuable brain time and energy. Therefore, failure to have the conviction—or courage—to make difficult decisions is often more damaging than making a bad decision. Once we understand this premise, we can free ourselves up to eliminate these obstacles to leadership.

PROCRASTINATION IS THE GREATEST OBSTACLE TO LEADERSHIP.

However, overcoming these leadership blockades is often easier said than done. Following are a few tips to help break the logjam that procrastination can create.

ADMIT THE TRUTH.

The first key to overcoming procrastination and taking on difficult decisions is to admit that you have them to make. We find all kinds of ways to justify avoiding a decision: we don't have time; this isn't the right time of year; we're too busy to make waves. Identify those decisions you have been putting off, regardless of the reason, and ask yourself why. What is it about this decision that makes it so difficult to make? Once you identify the issue and admit it exists, you are better able to deal with it. You can't fight a demon you can't identify.

DETERMINE THE REAL OBSTACLE.

One-third of the battle is identifying the demon. The second third is determining why it is a demon in the first place. What is it about the decision that makes us avoid it? Are we apprehensive of the potential consequences? Are we avoiding a confrontation? Is it potentially embarrassing? Whatever the reason, it is important to know what about this decision is causing us to avoid it. Once we identify the cause, we can then address the final third of the equation—dealing with it.

OVERCOME THE OBSTACLE.

When you have difficult decisions to make, particularly personnel decisions, they eat at you. And you may not know it, but they could be costing you a great deal more. Your other employees often see that you have not taken action, and they wonder why. If they don't know the reason, they'll make up one of their own. Favoritism? Nepotism? Lack of backbone? It doesn't matter if it's true. Perception becomes reality, if it's not corrected. The only way to overcome the negative of procrastination is to act on the issue. You can justify your way out of it all day long, but it won't solve the problem. Do something, even if it is wrong!

No matter what kind of executive superman or superwoman you are, each of us has only so much energy we can develop and consume in a single day. When we use it up avoiding decisions, we can't use it doing what we need to be doing—leading. The best way to deal with a difficult decision is to make it. When we fail to do so, we clog our own systems, creating more problems for ourselves and for those around us.

When we act, even in difficult situations, we are leading by example. Our people are watching everything we do, determining how they will deal with a similar situation. When we free ourselves to act, we free our employees to do the same.

Asking the Right Questions at the Right Time

AUTHOR JOHN GARDNER SAID in his book *Excellence: Can We Be Excellent and Equal Too?* "Most ailing organizations have developed a functional blindness to their own defects. They are not suffering because they cannot resolve their problems, but because they cannot see their problems."

Very often, we are victims of our own successes. What I mean by that is that sometimes we become so comfortable with our accomplishment that we don't dare question how it happened. After all, why would we want to change something that works?

The sign of true leadership is a willingness to challenge success in the same way we would challenge failure. Jack Welch, the legendary leader of GE, says his operating theory is that someone, somewhere has a better idea or a better way to do something, and the organization's top priority must be to search out those ideas and implement them where prudent.

Enlightened leaders have an ability to see things before they become obvious. After all, when the roof is leaking, it doesn't take much skill to know the roof needs to be repaired. The key is to have enough vision, and insight, to know the roof needs to be fixed before it becomes obvious, before it begins to leak and cause other damage.

So, how do we stay ahead of the curve? How do we avoid that functional blindness that comes when we are dazzled by our own successes or unwilling to admit there may be a better idea somewhere else that could help our organizations?

UNDERSTAND THE IMPORTANCE OF CHALLENGING OUR BELIEFS, BUT ON THE HEELS OF SUCCESS, NOT JUST IN THE AFTERMATH OF FAILURE.

The old adage says the best time to make a big sale is right after a big sale. High achievers don't rest after success—they double their efforts. Don't fall into the trap of waiting until something is broken before you begin to think about fixing it. Have the vision to ask "why" when things go right, as well as when they go wrong. The only thing more dangerous than not understanding what went wrong is not knowing what went right.

HIGH ACHIEVERS DON'T REST AFTER SUCCESS—THEY DOUBLE THEIR EFFORTS.

UNDERSTAND WHAT YOU ARE CHALLENGING.

So often when we look back at our efforts, we are stuck on asking "how" we got where we did. The truth is, our time might be better spent by focusing on "why" we got where we did. The actions we take very often are not as important as the motivation that led us to take them in the first place. Remember the discussion about being "blinded" to our shortcomings? You may be the best brain surgeon in the world, but if the patient has a heart problem, you probably aren't going to be much help. Being good at what we do is only effective when we are doing what needs to be done. When we are so focused on evaluating whether "we did it right," we often miss the fact that we may not have been doing the right thing. This is when the leader must effectively communicate his or her vision throughout the organization.

UNDERSTAND THE DEFINITION OF SUCCESS.

To take my previous point a bit further, it is critical that everyone in the organization is on the same page when it comes to defining success. Often we hear employees say, "Hey, I did my part. I can't help it that 'they' didn't come through." When your organization is full of people who understand that success is defined by organizational accomplishment and not just departmental or individual accomplishment, then you have developed the kind of "ownership" mentality so prevalent in successful organizations. Enlightened leaders help their people see the importance of doing the right thing as opposed to doing things right. The process is important, but only when the result of the process meets or exceeds customer expectations.

Most things that "break" have been weakened over time, and the same process occurs in our organizations. By being the kind of leader who continually seeks out what might need repairing before it breaks, we can not only prevent more substantive damage before it occurs but promote a very healthy "skepticism" about our success that allows us to challenge everything and ask the question, "is there a better way?"

Have the vision and courage to ask questions when no one else thinks it's necessary.

Leadership is Not a One-Person Job

I AM FORTUNATE TO BE ABLE TO raise my three young boys in a rural setting in Texas, where we operate, among other things, a goat-breeding operation. To help us move feed and hay around the place, we have an electric utility vehicle (a golf cart with a dump bed). It comes in handy in a number of different ways.

My wife and I recognized one of those ways very early in the life of our oldest son, Clayton. When we had a difficult time getting him to sleep, Clayton and I would drive around in that cart, and he would literally fall asleep in my arms. By the time he was five years old, I had watched him grow up in that seat next to me. He loved that cart. Nearly every day, we simply loaded up his younger, twin brothers, and we rode around our place.

One day, though, we reached a milestone. I was gone for the weekend, and my wife, Jill, allowed Clayton to sit in her lap and steer the cart. From that point forward, as you can imagine, he developed a new fire in his belly to drive the cart himself. Obviously, because he was age five, we didn't turn over the keys to him. But now we do let him steer the cart on a regular basis.

A curious thing happened through all this. It is not unusual for me to come outside now and find him working on the cart—cleaning it, checking the air pressure in the tires, and so on. He has literally taken ownership of this vehicle, because he now gets to drive it as opposed to just riding in it. This can be a valuable lesson for all of us.

Recently, I read in an industry publication about the importance of the leader of any organization exhibiting a number of admirable traits. And while the article made some good points, I think it failed overall, because it promoted the concept that there is *one* leader in any organization and that the *one* leader is solely responsible for vision, enthusiasm, encouragement, etc.

The truth is, in effective and successful organizations, every single person has the opportunity to be a leader. Sure, someone ultimately sitting at the top of the organizational chart may have the final say. But true leaders who are getting the most out of the people in their organizations allow each and every person the opportunity to contribute as a leader.

Do you have this kind of empowering environment in your company or your department? Or are you the "boss," and everyone knows it?

The days of the "boss" are over. As Thomas Friedman writes in his book, *The World Is Flat*, organizations have become more lateral and less vertical. The days of a boss sitting in a perch above the assembly line and looking for things to go wrong are long gone. Leadership occurs from the front of the line, not above it.

ARE YOU GIVING YOUR PEOPLE THE
OPPORTUNITY TO DRIVE THE CART
INSTEAD OF JUST RIDING IN IT?

Now is the time to take a close look at your organization and ask yourself if you are allowing every single person the opportunity to be a leader. Are you giving your people the opportunity to drive the cart instead of just riding in it? The story of my son Clayton is a perfect, if not simplified, example of how we naturally take ownership of a process when we have a sense of charting our own course instead of depending on someone else to steer.

I challenge you as a leader to turn over the wheel to your employees. Sure, you still have the opportunity and the need to put on the brakes or even hit the accelerator from time to time. And if things get way off course, you can always help get them back on track.

Great organizations are made up of many leaders. When we create an organization or a department made up of people who are willing and able to take the wheel instead of just going along for the ride, we create an entire legion of dedicated employees willing to take ownership of the process.

So, as you move into the next few weeks, step back and ask yourself what you are doing to grow more leaders instead of more followers. When you truly are successful in handing the wheel to your people, you are providing the kind of leadership that will pay off for you, your organization, your people, and your customers. And that sounds like a win-win situation to me.

One Eye on Today, One Eye on the Future

OUR THREE SONS ARE A JOY to both Jill and me. But I have to admit they are a handful. As a matter of fact, they are four handfuls at most times. I find myself, especially with the twins, wishing my optic muscles were not interconnected so that I could follow one child with one eye and the second with my other eye. It sure would look odd, but I'm convinced it would make me a more effective parent.

I think many of us could use the same talent in our business. Enlightened leaders have the ability to strategically multitask to keep one eye on today's challenges and the other on the future.

How is it possible to effectively do both? Following are a few strategies for helping leaders make the decisions today that will pay off in the future.

CREATE A FORMAL PROCESS.

Strategic planning does not happen by accident. To be able to plan for tomorrow in the midst of today's challenges requires discipline. Schedule time personally, and as a group, to escape the day-to-day tasks for the specific purpose of strategic planning. To be effective, participants have to be able to clear their minds of today's problems in order to think creatively about how to deal with the future.

TO BE ABLE TO PLAN FOR TOMORROW
IN THE MIDST OF TODAY'S CHALLENGES
REQUIRES DISCIPLINE.

UNDERSTAND BUSINESS CYCLES.

Most business trends are cyclical. What goes up usually comes down. By examining the trends in our own business and economy, we can be better prepared for what is coming next. So often, we wait until the storm looms on the horizon to build a roof on the house. In fact, we know well that sooner or later it is going to rain—so why not build that roof now? When we learn from the past, we can be better prepared to deal with the future. Plan now and control the issue instead of waiting until change is imminent and reacting defensively.

MAKE A LIST AND CHECK IT OFTEN.

Just like Santa Claus, we should make a list and check it twice. When your mind is clear and you are thinking straight, make a list of warning signs to identify problems that may be developing in your business and then pay attention to what is happening around you. For instance, on a very basic level, changing accounts receivable aging is a significant business indicator. Longer pay cycles could mean less accuracy in billing, which could indicate a personnel issue in that department or a problem with a process or a technology tool. Because you are not involved daily in that department, it might be a long time before you would personally witness a personnel problem or an IT issue. However, by paying attention to that key indicator—AR aging—you are able to effectively address a brewing storm before it becomes a raging flood.

LEARN FROM OTHERS.

I believe benchmarking against others—not just those in your industry, but against any business with a specific organizational skill set—is very valuable. For instance, if you want your company to be better at customer service, benchmark against the companies that are best at it, companies like

Southwest Airlines, Lands End, Dell Computing, and others. We often make the mistake of benchmarking against our competitors. That is fine and can be valuable, but our competitors might not be any better at certain tasks than we are, and all we are doing is finding out how we compare with others, not how we compare with the best. And don't just look for what companies do right. Pay attention to what they do wrong as well. There are valuable lessons to be learned in other people's failures. By benchmarking and studying best practices, you can get valuable direction on where and how you want to be in the future.

Leaders, by definition, have to be effective multitaskers. We have to disconnect our business optical nerves so our eyes can go in (at least) two different directions at one time, focusing on multiple targets. The challenges are simply too great to put all our attention in one area.

The Key to a Positive Attitude

ATTITUDE IS REAL. It is not a word from a self-help book. It is not a concept to be preached about when morale is down. Attitude is the very platform on which we stand. It impacts how we feel, how we act, and how we react—and, most importantly, it impacts our ultimate effectiveness as leaders.

Great leaders have great attitudes. That attitude may not manifest itself in a bubbly, slap-you-on-the-back kind of personality. Instead, attitude in leadership is more about our outlook. When we have a positive outlook, we have hope when others give up. We see opportunities where others see obstacles. We see learning experiences where others see failure. We see and focus on what is right about people instead of getting bogged down in what is wrong.

WE SEE LEARNING EXPERIENCES
WHERE OTHERS SEE FAILURE.

Yet, every day, we are faced with challenges that often make it difficult to maintain a positive attitude. And when our attitude sours, our vision becomes obscured. We all know that vision—the ability and willingness to see the preferred outcome—is a critical trait for successful leadership. So, how do we maintain a positive attitude when life throws us a curve? How do we consistently portray an attitude that will help us turn lemons into lemonade? The answers to these questions are deep inside, but within reach, of each and every one of us.

Having a positive attitude requires a decision on our part; attitude is a choice, not a destiny. We choose our attitude, and we choose to maintain a positive attitude. In fact, situations in life are not negative—it is our interpretation of these situations that makes them negative. You've heard of always looking on the bright side? There is validity to the concept.

It is exciting to realize that we are all in control of our attitudes. We are in control of what we think, and no one can force us to give up that control. We most need a positive attitude in the midst of our challenges, when things are most hectic and it seems everything is going wrong.

Following are a few reminders to help you make the decision to stay positive.

LOOK FOR WHAT IS RIGHT AT ALL TIMES.

What we focus on becomes our reality. When we focus on what is wrong, we get more of it. This doesn't mean we should ignore our problems; it means we should acknowledge our problems and then focus on solutions. When we spend our time and energies focusing on solutions, we are making a conscious decision to be positive. Let go of the problem and get to the solution. The same goes for our people. We can always find something wrong with our people, but what does that accomplish? As leaders, we should look for what is good and right in our people, even in the most challenging times. Doing so will make a difference in how we respond to the challenges they bring to us or put on us.

PLAY THE CARDS YOU ARE DEALT.

We can spend all day complaining about the cards we are dealt when we should be focusing on a strategy of how to play the cards. Many a bad attitude has been born out of a feeling of helplessness, a feeling that we are victims. We are not. No matter the situation, regardless of how bad it may seem, we are in control and need to put our energies into what will happen from that point forward. Big money has been won at poker tables all across the land with terrible cards in hand. Those winning players chose to make the best out of the cards they were dealt and, in many cases, used strategy to overcome the hand they were holding. When you allow yourself to be controlled by a feeling of helplessness, you are giving up your choice to have a positive outlook.

SPREAD THE LIGHT, NOT THE DARK.

Your people are watching everything you do and say, whether you know it or not. When you are negative, you give your people permission to be negative. By remaining positive, even in the most challenging times, you are impacting many more attitudes than just your own. Again, this doesn't mean you have to walk around singing a song when your house is on fire. But it does mean that you should remain in control, understand the impact of your actions (and reactions), and remain solution oriented.

PUT ON THE BRAKES.

A positive attitude takes work. When you feel yourself becoming negative—in thought, word, or deed—simply tell yourself to stop. Put on the brakes yourself; don't wait for someone else to ask you what is bothering you. You are in control of everything about your attitude. Maintain that control, exercise it, and make it a tool in your arsenal.

Don't become a victim of the world. You are defined not by what happens in your life but by how you deal with it.

Focus the Flame

SET YOUR SIGHTS ON WHAT MATTERS MOST

IT'S NOT WHAT YOU LOOK AT THAT
MATTERS; IT'S WHAT YOU SEE.

HENRY DAVID THOREAU

Focusing on What Matters

A S I SAID EARLIER, what you focus on, you get more of. That goes for good things as well as bad, which is why a leader has to pay careful attention to focus and understand the implications of his or her actions. Remember, people are watching your every move to determine how they should act in similar situations. Your focus is contagious.

When developing company goals and objectives, it is important to focus on the items we want more of. For example, we don't want to reduce accidents; we want to increase accident-free operations. We don't want to reduce employee turnover; we want to improve employee retention. We don't want to eliminate bad debt; we want to improve on-time payment and collections. The difference is subtle but very significant.

WE DON'T WANT TO REDUCE
ACCIDENTS; WE WANT TO INCREASE
ACCIDENT-FREE OPERATIONS.

Look at the messages you are sending as a company and as a leader. Are you constantly talking about, and therefore focusing on, what is wrong? Or are you focused on the desired outcome, what you want *more* of? Are you a forward-looking company, or are you constantly reminding your people what they are doing wrong? It is much easier to focus on the problems, because they are obvious, and more difficult to focus on the solutions, because they may not be as easy to identify. And when solutions do reveal themselves, they sometimes require difficult decisions to implement. Quite simply, it is easier to focus on the problem instead of the solution.

One of the most discouraging aspects of meetings in today's business environment is that we spend a significant amount of time talking about *what* is wrong, casting blame for *who* was wrong, and often debating *why* they were wrong. Efficient and effective leaders quickly establish the objective (identify the problem) and then spend the bulk of the meeting focusing on the solution. Leaders don't let meetings get bogged down with the past; they keep their eye on the ball and keep the ball in front of them. Once the ball is past, it is too late.

As a leader, the challenge is simple: we must learn from the past, learn from what went wrong, and then *let go of it*. Focus on the solution—on what we want more of—and on the desired outcome. The best companies in business today are forward thinking, but more importantly, they are forward focused and solution oriented.

Creating a solution-oriented work environment provides our people with a target, a finish line. And as I like to say, racehorses run harder when they have the finish line in sight. To turn your thoroughbreds loose, give them an objective to focus on, point them in the right direction, and let 'em run!

Managing What Really Matters

ONE ESPECIALLY BEAUTIFUL Saturday morning, a young mother and father stood looking out the kitchen window. Their energetic little four-year-old son was playing in the yard and rolling around with one of his friends in a new patch of Bermuda grass. The father yelled out the window to the boys, "Get off that new grass, and go play somewhere else."

The mother turned to her husband and said, "What are you doing? Why can't they play there?" The father replied, "I'm trying to grow that grass. It'll never grow as long as they are playing on it." Mom responded quite simply, "We're not raising grass. We're raising a son."

What are you raising in your company? What are your managers focusing on? What are you focusing on? Is it really the important things?

We often get caught up in managing instead of leading. We have to do both. However, management provides short-term direction to your employees, while leadership results in long-term actions. Our actions should be more focused on leading than managing, but when we do manage, we shouldn't get caught up in the little things so much but should instead stay in tune with the big picture.

Management is what happens when we are in the room. Leadership manifests itself after we leave the room. Any wise employee will do what the boss says when the boss is there. But what happens when the boss leaves or isn't paying attention? This is where the results of leadership become critical.

As leaders, it is vital that we have clear and achievable goals and objectives for reaching these goals. True leaders stay focused on the goals and objectives and don't get caught up in the little things. That doesn't mean a leader doesn't pay attention to the details of everyday business. It does mean that a leader gets involved in those details that really matter.

A LEADER GETS INVOLVED IN THOSE DETAILS THAT REALLY MATTER.

For instance, maybe an employee is routinely late to work. You, being the leader you are, believe in a strong work ethic; you are always early and stay late. It really bothers you that this employee just won't get to work on time.

As a leader, you can't be "bothered." The issue is not that you get to work on time and the employee doesn't. The real issue is the impact the employee's tardiness has on the rest of the team and, ultimately, productivity. Quite frankly, if it is not having a negative impact on anyone but you, you should get over it. However, more likely than not, it is having a negative impact on the employees that see it. In this case, the employee should be counseled about the ramifications of his or her actions.

Any time we deal with the folks who work for us, we have to remember our job. It is not to show them who's in charge. It is not to "get back" at someone for past sins. It is simply to remedy the situation in a way that results in a win-win for everyone, including the employee, you, and, most importantly, the organization. To do that, you have to stay focused on the big picture, on the goals and objectives, and not on whether or not you "like" the employee or the employee's actions. As much as possible, keep emotion and personal feelings out of leading.

Next time you are walking around among your employees (which I hope you do regularly), and you see something that bothers you, stop and ask yourself if it really matters. How does it impact the organization? Just because it's not the way you would do it doesn't particularly make it bad. More importantly, it may not matter at all in the big picture.

Great leaders know their roles. They understand the difference in growing grass and raising children. They understand the difference in managing and leading. And most importantly, they understand that a supportive comment, in tune with the company objectives, is much more helpful than an off-hand criticism about something that "bothers" them but ultimately just doesn't matter.

Always remember your company's goals, and keep your actions in line with achieving them.

The Biggest Need Demands the Most Attention

WHAT DOES YOUR ORGANIZATION need more than anything? Notice the word is "need" and not "want." As a leader, you must be willing and able to answer this very key and central question.

Every person, every organization, every entity, whether human or corporate, has a core need. A need so great that it trumps everything else. A need so relevant that all other needs are secondary. A need so critical that, without the fulfillment of that need, success is not only unlikely but nearly unattainable.

So I'll ask it again: what is the core need of your business?

By the way, the answer is not more profit; profit is a byproduct of the core need. The answer is not more volume; volume is a byproduct of the core need. The answer is not growth; you guessed it—growth is also a byproduct of the core need.

If indeed more profit is needed, the core need of your business is what it takes to produce more profit. The same goes for volume or growth. In your organization, only you and your people can answer the question.

Part of any strategic planning process should be to identify this most important core need and then to direct every asset of the organization to meeting the need. From budgeting to personnel, the institutional focus of your business should be squarely on this target. How do you make sure you have that focus where it needs to be?

THE FIRST CHALLENGE IS TO IDENTIFY THE CORE NEED.

It may seem simple. But just as we often mistake symptoms for the illness, we have to be sure we are identifying the core need and not the byproduct of that need. For instance, our greatest need may be better communication. That communication could be key in helping achieve a number of goals, all leading to profits, more business, growth, etc. Without better communication, profits, new business, or growth may very well not be attainable. Therefore, the need is better communication, not the byproduct. Make sure you are treating the illness and not the symptoms.

> BE SURE WE ARE IDENTIFYING THE
> CORE NEED AND NOT THE
> BYPRODUCT OF THAT NEED.

ONCE YOU KNOW THE CORE NEED, USE ALL YOUR FIREPOWER TO HIT THE TARGET.

If something is important enough to be at the top of your list, it deserves your full attention. Often, our greatest need has attained that lofty position because it is a need that is difficult to meet. Many times, this occurs because we internalize the issue and try and solve it ourselves. Great leaders surround themselves with great people. Use all your assets, including your people, to address the need, and you will have a much better chance of reaching the goal. Don't try and fight the battle yourself.

CONTINUE TO RE-EVALUATE YOUR CORE NEED.

When you put enough focus on addressing an issue, it is likely that issue will be solved. The need will be met. When that happens, some other need will rise to the top of the list. Great leaders are constantly re-evaluating the needs of the organization and directing assets where they are needed. Don't take your eyes off the prize, but don't be afraid to move on to the next core need. Needs change, and so should your strategy for meeting them.

Of all the important things in your business, something simply has to be the most important. You have to know what that is and be willing and able to deal with it. You must include your people in the process, and you have to know when it is time to move on to something else.

Make sure that what you are focused on is what most needs your focus. That is true leadership.

Company Goals and Objectives are a Waste of Time

DON'T WASTE YOUR TIME on goals and objectives for your company. They are ineffective and don't work. That's right—they are a waste of your time.

This concept will either intrigue you to read further or will cause you to throw this book away. But this concept is not as heretical as you might think.

The truth is that your business can't accomplish anything. It has no ability to accomplish objectives or meet goals. In fact, your business is useless … on its own. The power of any business or organization is in its people. So when it comes to establishing objectives and goals, the focus should be on your people and not on your business.

Any time we are involved in the strategic process of setting priorities, objectives, and goals, we should abandon the thought that we can "control" anything. What we should strive to do is "impact" the three key areas below if we want the results to show in our business in the form of efficiency, consistency, and, ultimately, profitability.

OURSELVES.

Our personal priorities, objectives, and goals should be in line with what we want our people and our business to accomplish. It is unrealistic to think we can produce major changes in our business without changing something about ourselves. It may be as simple as changing our own priorities, although it may also take more effort, more focus, more sweat…more whatever. The point is, if we want different results on the back end, we have to have different effort on the front end—and it all starts with us as individuals.

OUR PEOPLE.

You already know where I stand on the issue of business goals and objectives. There is absolutely nothing wrong with developing business goals and objectives in your mind, but they must be translated into goals and objectives for your people if they are ever to come to fruition. For example, if the goal is a 2 percent improvement in operating ratio, then how does that relate to the individual departments and the people in those departments? What will I, as your employee, need to focus on and accomplish if we are to make the business goals and objectives a reality? If you can't translate the goals down to the individual departments and people, then you haven't established specific and realistic goals and objectives.

OUR CUSTOMERS.

Many organizations leave this part out when they plan. Whether our customers ever know they are part of the process, impacting our customers gives us a much better chance of producing the results we need. Nothing more directly impacts our profitability than our customers. Why not have goals and objectives specific to them? For instance, if our company provides a service that is costly and not a core competency, yet our customers have come to expect it, why not create an objective to change that customer expectation and thereby eliminate a cost variable?

Effective leaders and organizations have written battle plans. Taking ideas from your head to paper is a valuable exercise that often helps clarify and solidify the plan. If you find you can't narrow it down to finite details, you don't have a good plan.

YOUR BUSINESS IS NOT YOUR ASSET;
THE PEOPLE WHO WORK IN
YOUR BUSINESS ARE.

Remember, you can't control anything but yourself. However, as a leader, you can impact a great many things and people. Your business is not your asset; the people who work in your business are. Don't develop a plan to make your business successful, but instead develop one to help your people and your customers be successful—and your business will benefit.

Balancing Time Between Good and Bad

F AR TOO OFTEN IN OUR ORGANIZATIONS, it is the people and issues that least deserve our attention that ultimately receive the most of it. Or, in more simple terms, we spend so much time as leaders dealing with problems that we are often too emotionally—and sometimes too literally—distracted to provide support and reinforcement for the people and projects that are running smoothly.

The question becomes: how do we balance our time and efforts so that we are not spending time acknowledging and even encouraging disruptive and negative behavior but instead are supporting positive behavior and results?

The truth is that whatever we focus on uses up our resources, both mental and physical. So when we spend considerable time dealing with negative behavior and problems, not only do we plant the seed that this type of behavior gets attention, but we also use up our resources in a way that can emotionally sour and even drain us. When that happens, we don't have time to spend on what we should be paying attention to.

I BELIEVE THAT WHATEVER WE
FOCUS ON, WE GET MORE OF—
EVEN IF IT IS NEGATIVE.

I believe that whatever we focus on, we get more of—even if it is negative. Therefore, it is critical that we, as leaders, find a way to not get bogged down with what's wrong but instead make it a top priority to focus more on what is right—so we get more of what is right.

Let's face it: we all have to deal with problems. When the alarm rings, we have to answer it. And we will; that's how we got where we are. However, enlightened leaders understand the importance of spending as much or more time practicing fire prevention as fire fighting. How can we all maintain that important balance?

MANAGE YOUR RESOURCES BETTER.

Our greatest resources as leaders are our own time and attention. No one can manage these for us, so we have to be responsible and accountable for how we allocate them. We often know when we are spending (wasting) our time in ways we shouldn't, and we are the only ones who can do something about it. If you wait for problems to go away, you will be waiting for a long time. Manage your time. It is yours, not your employees'. Not your customers'. Not your vendors'. Manage your time and attention better, and you will manage and lead your people better.

APPLY YOUR OWN BALANCE BRAKES.

If during a day you find you have spent the entire morning on problems, make a decision to call a time-out (within reason) and move your resources in the direction of more positive activity. It may be as simple as leaving your office and walking through the area with positive comments and encouragement for your people. By doing so, you give yourself an emotional time-out from the problems and also provide valuable affirmation to people in your organization who are not presenting problems. Again, if your people perceive that the only way they can get your attention is to have a problem, then— guess what?—they'll come up with problems (real or not) to get your attention.

DEAL WITH THE REAL ISSUE.

As I have said, procrastination is the biggest enemy of leadership. How much of your time is used dealing with problems over and over again? We don't get burned out dealing with issues; we get burned out dealing with the same issues time and time again. When we deal with the cause of a problem instead of the symptoms of it, we do everyone a huge favor. If you seem to be going around and around on the same issue, stop and determine if you are really dealing with the root of the problem or if you are attempting to dance around the edges. We often know what needs to be done but fail to pull the trigger. It can be lonely at the top. Leaders carry an additional burden. When you fail to act, it not only impacts you but others in your organization. By not wasting time on the fluff, you can get to the meat of the matter and then refocus on more positive activities.

We are all human. We can only take so much bad news and frustration, especially in one day. You could easily spend your entire time at work, and maybe at home, putting out fires. Make the decision to share your time between fire prevention and fire fighting, and you will be a better leader for it.

Creating a Complaint-Friendly Organization

I LOVE THE CARTOON THAT DEPICTS a manager standing in front of a customer service slide presentation showing a graph that trends abruptly downward. The caption below it reads, "I am pleased to announce that the number of customer complaints has dropped dramatically since doing away with the complaint form." The situation, while comical, actually rings true and reminds us, as leaders, how we have to be very careful to make sure we are asking our people to produce what we really need—results.

Many companies include performance objectives that involve reducing and/or eliminating customer complaints. The intention, obviously, is to reduce service failures. However, we have it completely backwards when we focus more on eliminating complaints than on service failures. That concept would be like a city reducing its crime statistics by eliminating the 9-1-1 phone system. You can't solve a crime you never know about. And in our situation, you can't deal with a complaint you never hear about.

In my opinion, in fact, complaints are a very valuable gift from our customers—both internal and external. When we focus on reducing or eliminating complaints, we are greatly hindering our ability to respond to our customers.

The question to ask yourself is, "Do I have a complaint-friendly organization?" Have you created an atmosphere that welcomes feedback, even negative feedback, from your customers? Do your people look at complaints as an opportunity to excel as opposed to a situation that requires a justification or even deflection of blame? Is the philosophy of your department or company, "No news is good news?"

DO YOUR PEOPLE LOOK AT COMPLAINTS
AS AN OPPORTUNITY TO EXCEL
AS OPPOSED TO A SITUATION
THAT REQUIRES A JUSTIFICATION
OR EVEN DEFLECTION OF BLAME?

Imagine a business environment in which we are allowed only one mistake per customer. Where we have to get it right the first time or the customer takes his or her business elsewhere. What would we do if we had no opportunity to deal with service failures that we know are ultimately going to happen?

The attitude with which we deal with complaints is vital. We know that the attitude we take into a situation often determines the outcome. What is your response when the phone rings? Do you welcome the call, even knowing that there is a distinct possibility there is a problem on the other end of the line? The truth is, if we never had problems in our business and, thus, the phone never rings, most of us would not have a job. We are here to solve problems. That is the nature of business, especially in the service sector, and we should have the right attitude about dealing with problems and the way they are communicated—very often through verbal complaints.

The simple fact of the matter is, a complaint is the expression of an expectation that has not been met. Nothing more, nothing less. A complaint is, most times, not a personal attack. It is not an attempt to ruin your company. It is certainly not a bother—if you have the right attitude. A complaint is an opportunity to close the "expectations gap" that has been created by the service failure and an opportunity to build a long-term customer.

Things are going to go wrong; it's inevitable. Our organizations will be known for how we deal with these situations when they occur. Our customers want to know how much we care. Sure, the price is important. But what customers want to know is that, when things go awry, we are open to feedback and willing to address the situation with a positive attitude.

Having a complaint-friendly organization is not easy or simple. It takes discipline. It takes training. It takes an understanding of what our jobs really are. Enlightened leaders welcome the opportunity to respond to complaints and use the process as a chance to get better; they do not use the information to "find out who screwed up." A solution-oriented leader moves beyond what went wrong to determine what he or she can do to make it right.

When you and your people are open to complaints and look forward to closing the "expectations gap," you truly have created a complaint-friendly environment.

Tools for Creating a Complaint-Friendly Organization

COMPLAINTS, IF HANDLED CORRECTLY, give us the opportunity to build customers for life. Wanting to be complaint-friendly is one thing; making it happen is another. What tools can you use to develop a truly complaint-friendly organization?

FIRST AND FOREMOST, IT TAKES A COMMITMENT ALL THE WAY FROM THE TOP TO THE BOTTOM.

When the attitude about complaints is that they are an opportunity and not a problem, the process is well underway. However, it only takes one or two weak links in your organization to bust the system. We all have to deal with complaints from internal as well as external customers, and there is absolutely no room for some to buy into the concept and others not to.

THE NEXT KEY IS TO MAKE SURE PEOPLE UNDERSTAND THE IMPORTANCE OF NOT TAKING COMPLAINTS PERSONALLY.

Remember, a complaint is an expression of an unmet expectation. It is not a personal attack, and it is not a threat. No matter how it comes across verbally, a complaint is a gift we want from our customers. If something has to go wrong, we certainly want to know about it, so we can use it to get better.

IT IS CRITICAL TO KNOW WHAT YOUR CUSTOMERS WANT IF YOU EXPECT TO CONSISTENTLY DELIVER IT.

Some people just like to gripe and complain. A very valuable tool in a customer complaint situation is to ask the question, "What is it I can do to make this better for you?" Continuing to talk about what is wrong doesn't do anything but raise emotions. Make sure when you are working to find a solution that you know what it is your customer expects. You already have one problem caused by an unmet expectation, so make sure the second time around you and your customer are on the same page about what a "resolution" means.

UNDERSTAND THAT YOU CAN'T HELP THE IRATE.

The key to solving a customer service problem is to get past the emotion and focus on the real issues. When someone is upset or irate, you must make it clear that dealing with the issue is a top priority and an opportunity. Never transfer complaints from angry customers; take the responsibility to calm them down first, and then get them to the appropriate person. It is much easier to just transfer them right away, but nothing upsets already dissatisfied customers more than being put on hold. That just gives them more time to wish they were doing business with someone else.

UNDERSTAND THAT SAYING "I'M SORRY" IS NOT AN ADMISSION OF GUILT.

It simply means you're sorry the problem occurred. This is a great tool to calm customers and make them feel you are truly interested in helping them with their issue. That is the first challenge. Make sure they know you care. Anyone with any intelligence is not going to continue to beat on someone they believe is truly trying to assist them.

These tools can help in most situations. But some folks don't really want a solution; they just want to vent. Sometimes, the best thing is to let them do just that and then move on. Customer service is not science. It is an art, and each situation takes common sense and good judgment. Apply the golden rule, and you will often find your approach to a solution.

Great customer service takes time. Enlightened leaders understand the importance of each and every situation. We are not judged by what goes right; unfortunately, we are often labeled by what goes wrong...and how we deal with it.

OUR SERVICE IS OFTEN DEFINED
BY HOW WE DEAL WITH SITUATIONS
WHEN THEY GO WRONG.

Often, the only thing we have to set ourselves apart from our competitors is our service. More importantly, our service is often defined by how we deal with situations when they go wrong. Make sure everyone in the organization knows that the best chance to excel is when there are problems. Using these potentially negative situations to grow customer confidence, looking at them as opportunities, and looking at every complaint as a gift are all ways to be sure your company is a complaint-friendly organization.

When We Try to Do Too Much

WHEN YOU GOT UP THIS MORNING, what was the most important thing on your to-do list? How long into the day did it take before you began to address that issue? Did you get sidetracked and never get to that issue at all? Even worse, did you begin work today without a to-do list?

One of the challenges today's leaders face is that we walk onto the battlefield every day and often have so many targets we don't know which one to shoot at first. Even when we do recognize the most important target, we often are distracted by secondary issues and don't give our primary target the attention it deserves. Do you ever find yourself in this situation?

Focus is a great thing for any manager or leader. However, to truly utilize focus to its fullest extent, we have to understand the reality of focus. That reality includes the following:

YOU CAN ONLY TRULY FOCUS ON ONE THING AT A TIME. We all have to multitask, but we must focus on an issue to give it the attention it deserves. Try this exercise the next time you walk outside: look out across the horizon, pick something out, and focus on it. Then try and focus on something else without losing focus on the first object. Can't do it, can you? It is impossible. Our eyes can only focus on one thing at a time. The same thing goes for our brains. To truly bring something into clear focus, we have to concentrate on it and it only for some period of time. When we try to take in too much at a time, we never take in any of it fully.

WHAT WE FOCUS ON, WE GET MORE OF.

This is true even if what we are focusing on are obstacles. When we get so focused on what is wrong in our business, we simply don't have the ability to focus on the solutions. That doesn't mean we ignore our problems. That does mean we should identify them, then let go of them, and put our focus on solutions. I believe one of the leading causes of frustration among business leaders occurs when they get too preoccupied with the obstacles and lose focus on the opportunities. Ask yourself if you really are solution-oriented or if you spend too much time blaming people for what is wrong. Get over it, and get on with it.

WHAT WE FOCUS ON, WE ACHIEVE.

When we ourselves focus on a particular task, and when we help our people focus on a particular task, we will work more consistently to achieve that task. It is the "light at the end of the tunnel" concept. When the destination is clearly in sight, we will work harder to get there. When we tell our people to just start running and that we'll tell them when to stop, they have no idea how hard to run. They don't know if they are traveling a hundred yards or a hundred miles. By providing a clear focus point, we greatly improve the chances that we will actually reach that point.

WE CAN OFTEN MULTITASK OUR
PEOPLE, AND OURSELVES,
RIGHT INTO MEDIOCRITY.

In business today, we often put significant value on people who are effective multitaskers. But the truth is, we can often multitask our people, and ourselves, right into mediocrity. We must resist the temptation to add more to the plates of our best people simply because they have been so effective. We must also resist the temptation to take on more ourselves than we can reasonably handle.

Focus is a powerful tool, but only when we understand its limitations and pitfalls. By helping our people focus on the right things, and allowing ourselves to focus on the right things, we really are providing quality leadership and helping ensure that we are accomplishing what is important in our lives. Don't try to do too much, or you will find yourself losing ground instead of gaining it.

The True Power of a Solution-Oriented Organization

I HAVE ADDRESSED THE IMPORTANCE OF DEVELOPING an organization that is solution oriented rather than problem oriented. Remember, what we focus on we get more of. So when we spend time on solutions, we are using our limited resources in the most efficient and effective way.

However, it is just as important to remember that *organizations* don't focus on anything; the people within them do. For your company to be solution oriented and forward thinking, each person, one at a time, must adopt and embrace the ability to focus forward like a laser.

It takes a certain level of maturity to understand the importance of *what* is right as opposed to *who* is right. When a majority of your people can grasp this very basic concept, a sort of organizational Nirvana occurs and allows your team to get beyond the blame game and on to the business of solutions and success instead of problems and frustration.

UNDERSTAND THE IMPORTANCE
OF WHAT IS RIGHT AS OPPOSED
TO WHO IS RIGHT.

How do we, as leaders, help eliminate the frustrations and wasted energy that come from putting more focus on our problems than on solutions? Here are a few ideas:

OBSERVE THE 80/20 RULE.

Any meeting, discussion, or internal brainstorming should spend no more than 20 percent of the time on what is wrong; the rest should be spent on the solution(s). A majority of workers responding to a recent survey indicated a high level of frustration with meetings because it seems much more time is spent on what is wrong instead of the solution. In fact, many indicated the conversation never even gets around to a solution; war stories and blame dominate many meetings. Don't let this happen in your organization. Get the issue or problem on the table, and then move on to the more forward-focused work of the solution.

DON'T MIX PROCESS WITH PERSONNEL.

One of the keys to maintaining a solution-oriented organization, ironically, is properly classifying the problem. We often confuse process issues with personnel issues. We spend valuable time in meetings and conversations trying to change a process, when we should really be making a personnel change, and vice versa. There is no greater waste of time than bringing a group of people into a meeting to discuss how to fix a problem that everyone in the room knows is a personnel issue. This misplaced focus creates substantial frustration and causes our people to disengage on issues, because they sense leadership is not willing to face the truth. Make sure you are honest with yourself about the real issue before you bring other people into a situation you probably should be addressing on your own.

FOSTER A WORK ENVIRONMENT THAT IS FORWARD FOCUSED.

Think of what occurs in your business, from work assignments to compensation, and make sure you are encouraging and rewarding activity that does indeed lend itself to a solution-oriented organization. Each person on the team should have a role in achieving success—however you define it. When you have people who are managing your people—in other words, people who are "watching" others to make sure they don't foul up—then you are actually encouraging your reports to be better at finding problems instead of solutions. Each person's role should be making something happen instead of trying to keep something from happening. This is the difference in leadership and control. We can't control our people, no matter how hard we try. However, we can lead them.

Leadership, by definition, is forward focused. If you are spending a substantial amount of time trying to figure out what went wrong, you are managing instead of leading. Both are important roles. However, the most critical skill you can develop is identifying which one you are doing at any given time. Simply by achieving this self-realization, you can become more solution oriented and help your people do the same.

When "Doing Your Job" Takes on a New Meaning

W E LEARN SOME OF OUR BEST leadership lessons from real-life experience. Recently, a friend and I had the opportunity to spend the weekend at a relatively new Arizona resort. Upon arriving, I pulled into the covered entrance in my rental car, where a small army of attendants, at least eight of them, awaited to greet me and park my vehicle. I'm not sure I had ever seen such a large, orchestrated, and inviting valet staff in my entire life.

I had no more stopped my vehicle when the troops descended on us, opening my door and the passenger door for the friend traveling with me. That was followed by an immediate, and I believe heartfelt, welcome from at least four of those assembled. Seemingly simultaneously, yet another uni-formed member of the resort Welcome Army was already retrieving our lug-gage from the trunk. In a matter of no more than ten seconds, our bags were unloaded, and we had officially arrived.

I immediately informed the attendant who appeared to be in charge that we were checking in but would be right back out and would need to leave again to go to the airport to pick up our wives. After retrieving my Blackberry that I had left in the car, I reminded the attendant once again that I would be right back out to go to the airport.

My friend and I went inside to check in and, while at the registration desk, we were approached by the valet captain, who handed me the valet ticket. I again reminded him that we would be right back out and needed the car so we could return to the airport.

Not more than two minutes later we returned to the entrance, where—to our incredible chagrin—we found that the car was gone. In fact, there were no cars in sight, and all eight attendants were repositioned, awaiting the next arrival.

We asked for our car and were told to go to the valet window and it would be retrieved. Just more than seven minutes later, our car was back, and we were on the way to the airport. As a result of the valet snafu, we were a few minutes late to the airport. We explained the story to our wives, which, thankfully, they accepted as a reasonable excuse for our tardiness.

When we returned to the resort, I asked for the manager on duty and, in the spirit of constructive feedback, told him what had happened. He apologized but explained that the valet team's main goal was to limit any congestion in the entrance area so there would be no delay for arriving guests. I thanked him for his time and returned to the entrance area, found the attendant who had welcomed me, and asked him politely what he did for the resort. He made it clear his job was to welcome guests and keep the entrance clear of congestion. "In other words, I park cars," he said. I congratulated him on doing his job in a very efficient and effective manner.

UNFORTUNATELY, HE WAS SO BUSY
DOING HIS JOB THAT HE DIDN'T LISTEN
TO THE CUSTOMER.

The only problem is that his job, in a service environment, is not to park cars. His job is to meet customer needs. He was doing exactly what he thought he was supposed to do. In fact, he was doing what he was trained to do: he kept the entrance clear and kept the cars moving. Unfortunately, he was so busy doing his job that he didn't listen to the customer. What happened is not his fault. What happened falls squarely on the shoulders of management.

When we put so much focus on tasks, rules, and regulations, we can cause our people to take their eye off the real prize, meeting customer expectations. We convince our people to get so focused on the trees that they fail to see the forest.

There is nothing wrong with task- or objective-oriented training, as long as one of the tasks or objectives is meeting overall customer expectations. We can be experts at a particular task and still not meet customer expectations. Being good at what we do only works if what we do is what the customer needs.

As leaders, we owe it to our people to never lose sight of the ultimate prize of meeting our customers' needs. The objective should not be to stay busy, unless we are busy doing those things that help us meet customer expectations while maintaining profitability. Our focus should not be on parking cars, when our customer doesn't need his car parked. We must keep the horse before the cart. If we, as leaders, maintain the proper perspective, we can help our people and our organizations focus on what matters.

Look at the people within your organization, and determine if they really understand their jobs. Are they busy parking cars? Are they so busy doing their jobs they don't do what ultimately needs to be done? Be clear with expectations, and results will follow. When objectives are results oriented instead of activity based, we are helping our people focus on the right things and doing our jobs as leaders.

Are You Creating Monsters Within Your Organization?

I HAVE CREATED A MONSTER in my young son Clayton. A virtual ticking time bomb I have on my hands. Focus on the ticking.

It all started the week we were fresh off a one-year run of the "Why, Daddy?" tour, during which my son would follow every single statement I made with his favorite response, "Why, Daddy?" Then came the "When are we going to be there?" phase. Every five minutes, from somewhere in the back seat would come the question, "When are we going to be there?" So, in our infinite wisdom, my wife and I decided it was time, no pun intended, to teach our son about the concept of time. Maybe not the best idea we've ever had.

As we wanted, the new focus of my five-year-old became time. He understood the concept but didn't get the math. When we were going to the store for groceries, he would ask, "How long until we get there?" and I would say, "A few minutes." His immediate response would be, "How long is a few?" When I would say ten minutes, he would ask, "How long is ten minutes?" I think you get the picture. All of a sudden, shifting the focus to time didn't seem like such a wonderful idea. As a matter of fact, in a move I am sure will not garner me the coveted "Parent of the Year" award, I then tried to abandon the entire concept of helping my son understand time.

The problem I had created was that, while I was attempting a hiatus from my time instruction, my son didn't care and wanted to know more. He didn't know or understand why I didn't want to talk about time anymore. He still wanted to know all about seconds and minutes and hours and days and…yes, even weeks, months, and years. I had started something, and I had an obligation to continue it.

How many times have we done the same thing in our organizations? For instance, we attend the weekly staff meeting and hear about a rash of billing errors. So what do we do? We put an emphasis on preventing billing errors. We may even invest in new technology or training to help our people with the problem. We get our people focused on the issue, and improvements are made.

Three weeks later, we attend the weekly staff meeting and find out we have experienced a rash of customer service failures. Now the focus is on customer service. We make sure everyone attends mandatory training on the subject. We put out memos about the importance of customer service and we harp on it, day after day, for a month. And just as the momentum seems to be turning and our employees make real strides in customer service, we have a new crisis of the month. The focus changes again. Sound familiar?

Unfortunately, many of us in leadership positions react the same way when a problem arises. We want all hands on deck to get the problem solved … until the next crisis unfolds. Then we want all the hands on deck working on that problem. But the truth is, our people are just getting their hands around the first crisis. Doesn't matter; we're ready for them to change their focus and address the latest crisis.

While this scenario is how business in real life works, it causes problems. And we as leaders are the only ones who can do anything about it. The next time you attend the latest and greatest seminar and come back to the office with an entire legal pad full of ideas, understand the importance of your people's perspective. You may be energized with new ideas, but they are still dealing with the crisis you handed them just before you left. You may be ready to change the focus, but they aren't there yet.

As leaders, we must multitask. We are juggling several balls all the time. We are supposed to; that's what we are paid to do. But our people often are not so inclined. Most people can effectively focus on only one thing at a time; maybe they can pay attention to several things at a time, but they can only focus on one. When we keep changing directions on them—changing focus—we leave them in a position of frustration, as in the time example with my son Clayton. He doesn't understand why I was a veritable font of information on time one week and then didn't want to talk about it anymore.

GREAT LEADERS UNDERSTAND THEY
CAN'T JUMP FROM ONE PRIORITY
TO ANOTHER AND EXPECT ANY ISSUE
TO ACTUALLY GET THE PROPER FOCUS.

Leaders finish what they start and, when they can't, take seriously the implications of not doing so. They understand the importance of consistency in actions and in thoughts. Great leaders understand they can't jump from one priority to another and expect any issue to actually get the proper focus.

And so I needed to finish what I had started with my son. We began to explore the concept of Christmas coming once a year. When I told Clayton he wouldn't be getting Christmas presents for a year, he asked, "How long is a year?" When I said, "Twelve months," he asked, "How long is twelve months?" When I said, "Fifty-two weeks," he asked, "How long is fifty-two weeks?" And on and on.

In the meantime, let's all work on our consistency as leaders and make sure we help our people focus on what is important to the organization and not just on what is on the top of our minds on a given day. Your business deserves it. Your customers deserve it. And your people deserve it.

Carry the Torch

LIGHT THE WAY FOR YOUR PEOPLE

IF YOU WANT TO BUILD A SHIP,
DON'T HERD PEOPLE TOGETHER
TO COLLECT WOOD AND DON'T
ASSIGN THEM TASKS AND WORK,
BUT RATHER TEACH THEM
TO LONG FOR THE ENDLESS
IMMENSITY OF THE SEA.

ANTOINE DE SAINT-EXUPÉRY

Understanding the Value of Character in Your Organization

L EGENDARY UCLA BASKETBALL COACH John Wooden has said many times that character is the most foundational trait of any human being. What I believe he meant was that, without character, traits such as talent and desire just don't matter that much. The most talented, technically proficient employee, without character, will be a liability to your team.

That being said, it is often very difficult to adequately judge a person's character by looking at her résumé or even through conducting an in-depth interview. Sure, there are trick questions and personality profiles and even methods to verify claims on the résumé. But determining character is often not so black and white. Character, as with much in life, involves a lot of gray area. Even the definition of character varies, depending on who you are talking to.

I think every leader wants to believe every person on his or her team has character. But what does that mean? Does it mean they are honest? Does it mean they believe in some firm set of standards? Does it mean they are a character?

For the sake of this discussion, I would like to propose that a person with character operates consistently within a set of generally acceptable standards and is ultimately guided by doing "the right thing." The dictionary calls it "moral firmness."

The question becomes, as leaders, how do we fill our organizations with persons of character? While the answer is not clear-cut, there are a few guiding principles to help us, both as suggestions and as precautions.

BE CAREFUL ABOUT THINKING YOU CAN CHANGE PEOPLE.
It is very difficult to alter the established behavior of adults. In more simple terms, it is very difficult to teach an old dog new tricks. Character is a definable trait. Lack of character is as well. Coach Wooden often told his assistants, when they were out recruiting new talent for UCLA, that character is a trait athletes arrive with and that they will likely leave UCLA with the same character, or lack thereof, they arrived with. And he was even talking about fairly impressionable young people—adults are far less impressionable and much less likely to change. What they come with is what you will likely have to work with.

CHARACTER IS A DEFINABLE TRAIT.
LACK OF CHARACTER IS AS WELL.

NEVER CREATE YOUR OWN CHARACTER PROBLEMS.
Great leaders never put their people in a position of having to compromise their character. In dealing with customers, both internal and external, we have opportunities every day to stretch or bend the truth. It may seem innocent and trivial when it happens, but then what? Today's exception becomes tomorrow's expectation. A small slip in character today becomes the new benchmark for tomorrow. How much is too much? The truth is, when we put our people in a position of compromising their character—in any way—we are creating more problems for our people, our organizations, and ourselves.

KNOW THAT ORGANIZATIONS HAVE CHARACTER AS WELL.
While every organization is a sum total of the people who comprise it, the truth is that companies take on an institutional character: "That's not the way we do things." "Our company doesn't stand for that." "We're known for doing it right." Make sure you, as a leader, know what your company's reputation is, both internally and externally, and that it agrees with what you want it to be. Just one note: the external perception of your organization is seldom wrong. It is more likely that if the external perception differs from

your own perception, you may be the one missing the boat, because you are too close to see the organization as it actually is. Regardless, know your company's reputation, and make sure it is what you want it to be.

TREAT CHARACTER LIKE TALENT AND EXPERIENCE WHEN SEARCHING FOR PEOPLE.

Hire people for character as much as for how much business they can bring you. And apply the same standards to your current employees. Jack Welch, the legendary leader at GE, says one of the hardest things to do as a leader is to move against someone who meets or exceeds their goals but does it in a way that may run counter to company standards. These are the kind of people who inspire comments like, "He's a little unorthodox, but he gets the job done," or "I wouldn't have done it that way, but hey, it works." Make sure you hold yourself to the same standards you expect out of your people, and you will be on the way to that organization of character. It is very easy to turn your head when the numbers are there. Don't fall into that trap. Consistency is important for any leader, especially when it comes to character and expectations.

John Wooden was one of the most successful coaches in college basketball history. By understanding that talent without character is a recipe for failure, he built a tradition of winning. With the same understanding, you can do the same within your organization. Great leaders see the entire picture and understand the role of character in every employee and the entire organization. With that kind of vision, success, however you define it, is much more likely.

Hiring the Right Person for the Right Job

HOW DOES ONE DEVELOP a senior manager or leader for a key position in his or her company? For that matter, how do you find the person to replace you? It is that basic premise I am often questioned about when I work with companies and their leadership. There is no greater challenge in business today.

Leaders often struggle with the question of whether to hire from the outside or promote from within. But that truly is not the first item to address. In fact, there are a number of issues to be addressed before even beginning the actual process of filling a position. And by the way, as with any leadership task, effectively dealing with these issues takes a significant level of self-evaluation and honesty. Where do we start?

First of all, we have to know what, or who, we are looking for. If not, how will we know when we find the right fit? The primary task should be stepping back and developing an *objective* and thorough review of what skills, experience, and personality are needed for the position. Notice the emphasis on the word "objective." This is often not easy to do. When we are close to a situation, we sometimes are blinded to the most obvious. In fact, there are some mistakes to avoid when creating an *objective* job description.

DON'T FALL INTO THE TRAP OF HIRING SOMEONE LIKE YOURSELF, EVEN IF YOU ARE TRYING TO HIRE SOMEONE TO REPLACE YOU.

The key is to seek an individual who fits the need. Remember the word "objective." As an example, if, after the objective review, you determine that the position calls for an aggressive, experienced, hands-on manager with a track record of quantifiable success and the ability to work well with investors, hire a person that fits that bill, even if you are not aggressive and don't particularly enjoy dealing with investors. Hire for the position, not the person you're replacing, even if it is you.

SPEAKING OF HIRING FOR THE POSITION, MAKE SURE YOU ARE HIRING FOR WHERE YOU WANT TO BE IN THE FUTURE AND NOT WHERE YOU ARE NOW.

Is growth important? Do you need a turnaround manager? Do you need a change in style? Is it the goal to simply maintain? All these are legitimate questions and needs, and catering to them can help ensure that the person you put in the new position can actually get you where you want to go. As NHL great Wayne Gretzky says, "Skate to where the puck is going to be." Also, don't try to fill a position that requires meeting strict goals and objectives with someone who has never had to meet those kinds of numbers. It doesn't matter how much he impresses you in an interview. If he hasn't been in a pressure-packed situation in which he had to meet performance criteria, such as in sales or recruiting, he is not likely to perform well and get you where you need to go.

MAKE SURE YOU ARE HIRING FOR
WHERE YOU WANT TO BE IN THE
FUTURE AND NOT WHERE YOU ARE NOW

UNDERSTAND THE DIFFERENCE IN A MANAGER AND A LEADER, AND KNOW WHAT YOU NEED FOR THE POSITION IN QUESTION.

Managers are very hands-on and can often perform the specific tasks called for in the department. Leaders, on the other hand, understand the importance of helping their folks achieve, and they provide the tools to do so. Very strong, hands-on managers are often not effective leaders, because they have a tendency to take over when challenges surface. Leaders stay on the course and empower their people to rise to the challenge. Occasionally you can find both in one person. However, enlightened leaders know they can personally only accomplish so much on their own, so they spend a great deal of their time helping those around them grow, both personally and professionally. Ultimately, great leaders spend less time guarding the specific trees and put more effort into protecting the forest as a whole.

As to the issue of hiring from within or seeking a qualified candidate outside your company, I go back to the word "objective." As long as you know what you are looking for, it really doesn't matter where the person comes from. However, if you are focused on harvesting the talent within your organization, it is important to have a process.

What if you have picked out someone within the company you are grooming for a future management or leadership position? How can you be fair both to that person and your organization? The truth is, it is very difficult to prepare a person for an unknown task. Simply saying, "This person has a future as an executive in our company" has limited value. Once that "future" has been better defined, you can more effectively prepare that person for the task.

A very significant danger arises when you lose your objectivity (there's that word again) when mentoring a person. Deciding that person has a future, even if you have a specific position in mind, is a dynamic process. Don't get so married to your decision that you become blind to the obvious—it might not work out the way you thought. Be willing to accept what develops. Don't keep trying to force a square peg into a round hole just to protect your judgment. Great leaders accept mistakes, learn from them, don't consider them failure, and move on with the experience tucked away for future reference. In fact, the more you learn about a person, sometimes the more there is not to like. Stay objective throughout the process, and constantly reevaluate your decision.

Leaders are a reflection of the folks they have around them, and leaders aren't afraid of losing their jobs to those people. Most importantly, great leaders know they always have to have a succession plan. If you're gone today, will the department or organization continue to operate smoothly? If you are doing your job as a leader, the answer will be yes.

Hiring people is easy. Hiring quality people who fit your needs takes a little more effort. No hiring decision is a sure bet, no matter how much work goes into it, so leaders take the information they have and make the best decision they can. Then they constantly monitor and reevaluate, knowing circumstances can change and often do. Follow your best *objective* instincts, and you will succeed much more often than not.

What Kind of Bullets
Are in Your Gun?

AS LEADERS, OUR ABILITY TO ACHIEVE is directly proportional to the quality of the people around us. Great leaders have great people working with and for them. Great leaders aren't afraid of hiring people who could replace them—in fact, they often hire people that could and would if given the chance.

The challenge to recruit and retain high-quality people has become so significant that I believe it has made us too dependent on the process of growing our own future leaders. How, you ask, could we have become too dependent? Because we are, many times, sending our people into a gunfight with a pocket knife. We simply don't do a good job of giving our folks the tools they need to succeed and, often, don't even utilize a fair and effective process to determine if they are up to the task.

We've all heard stories of promoting a great worker to the position of manager and finding that the person simply doesn't work out in the new role. Sometimes it's because we didn't provide the tools and training needed for that employee to take the next step. In other cases, the person just didn't have the skills or perspective to move from the role of a "doer" to the role of a "manager."

We have not been fair to that employee. We have set her up for failure. That is wrong for the employee, for the other employees she must work with, and for your business. Sure, you thought you were doing the right thing, or you wouldn't have made the move. But often our motivation is more out of desperation, something we don't always want to admit.

We have an opening, and we have an employee who has been doing a good job. We know that we probably should promote that employee, or the person may leave. One and one add up to two. But in truth, the equation is much more involved. We often don't give the kind of thought needed to the advancement of our people. In fact, some folks just aren't made to be managers. I know this sounds a bit cynical, but it's actually quite the opposite.

Entrepreneurial business leaders are often too loyal to their employees. We all probably know someone who should have been gone a long time ago, but the owner just won't let her go. And because she has hung on longer than most, somehow she keeps moving up the ladder. Sometimes it's not just *up* the ladder but "out" the ladder as well. We often try to isolate our problem people—put them in a small department where they don't have to interact with others—in an effort to do what's right. Not to be harsh, but I believe that, more often than not, that kind of misdirected loyalty does much more harm in the long run.

Jack Welch has produced more Fortune 500 leaders than anyone else in modern U.S. business history. In his book *Winning* he says, "Too many people work too hard to make Cs into Bs and As. It is a wheel spinning exercise. Identify your best people, give them the tools and training they need, reward them, promote them, and emotionally let go of the rest. Some people just aren't meant to manage."

It is very difficult to move against people in your organization who have been loyal. But it is a huge mistake to let those people move up the ladder, or even worse, force them up the ladder, just because we haven't done a good job, or are afraid, to seek quality people from the outside. Not having good pitchers in the bullpen can be a fatal mistake. Very few baseball teams have been successful growing their own talent, and the ones that have are very good at it. They have coaches with that task, they have systems, and they have scouts for situations when the help they need is on someone else's team.

What does your company's bullpen look like? Do you have coaches and systems to train your young talent? Are you so dependent on those currently on the team that you are blinded to who and what else is available? Do some people on the team need to be cut? Are you hurting your team in the name of loyalty?

These are all potentially difficult questions that you need to address. Whether you own the company or simply manage a department, as a leader, you owe it to your organization to shut the door, hold the calls, and ask yourself these questions. Who do I have around me? Am I being fair to everyone? Am I giving them the tools and training they need? Do I have the people in my organization who will help me achieve as a leader?

Make the decisions today that will make you and your organization successful tomorrow. Don't send your people into a gunfight with a pocketknife. Find out right now what kind of bullets you have in your company's gun. Great companies have great people! If you don't have them, go get 'em!

Developing the Team Around You

RALPH NADER ONCE SAID, "The role of a leader should be to develop more leaders, not more followers." Whether you agree with his politics or not, Nader is right on track when it comes to highlighting the role of the modern-day business leader. We are not generals leading troops into war, troops who are bound by regulations to follow our every command. No, our job as leaders is less about command and control and more about influence and persuasion.

Should you decide that the odds of success in obtaining quality people are greater when you put the focus on developing the people already around you, here are some ideas for helping you effectively "grow your own" leaders.

NARROW THE FIELD.

Not all people are meant to be bosses, and not all people want to be bosses. One of the keys to developing your own leaders is to first identify those within the organization who have potential in the form of talent *and* desire. Talent without desire is like a race car with no ignition—it doesn't matter how fast it will go, if you can't get it started. People have to be willing to do what it takes to become a leader. Leadership is not an assignment; it is a choice. When you can recognize who in your company at least has potential and is willing to use it, you are better able to monitor the progress those individuals are making.

> IF YOU DON'T HAVE SOME KIND OF FORMAL
> MEASURING STICK BY WHICH TO MEASURE
> THEIR PROGRESS, YOU LIKELY WILL BE
> MAKING YOUR DECISIONS BASED
> MORE ON YOUR PERSONAL LIKES
> AND DISLIKES ABOUT THE PEOPLE
> THAN ON THEIR QUANTIFIABLE RESULTS.

FORMALIZE THE PROCESS.

You have to get serious about developing your team; you can't only do it when it is convenient. Set specific goals and objectives for the individuals, even if they don't know what you are grooming them for. If you don't have some kind of formal measuring stick by which to measure their progress, you likely will be making your decisions based more on your personal likes and dislikes about the people than on their quantifiable results.

DON'T TRY TO MAKE EVERYONE AROUND YOU BE LIKE YOU.

We often want our people to treat our businesses the same way we do. And that is fine. But the truth is, people are different, and different leaders have different styles. In most cases, everyone does not have to travel the same road to reach a destination. To effectively grow your own leaders, what you really need to focus on is making your people understand the values of the company and the expectations placed upon them. They may have a different way of accomplishing their goals or objectives; in fact, they may have a better way to get there. So make sure you are focused on the right things. Just because they didn't respond to a situation exactly the way you would have does not, in and of itself, make their response wrong.

BE HONEST WITH YOURSELF AND YOUR PEOPLE.

If, during the process, you determine someone is not progressing or responding the way you hoped, deal with it. Don't procrastinate by "hoping" something will change. Your time is too precious to spend trying to turn a dirt clod into a diamond. Honest, non-emotional, and nearly continuous evaluation of your "prospects" helps ensure you are putting your efforts where they are most needed.

DON'T BE AFRAID OF LOSING THE GOOD ONES.

Jack Welch is widely known for developing leaders under his wing who went on to run Fortune 500 companies. That is one of the things he is most proud of. Yet I hear some executives say they hesitate to let some of their folks get involved in outside activities or attend advanced training, because all they are doing is becoming more marketable and attractive to other companies. So what? It should be the goal of every leader to have a building full of people that every competitor would like to hire. Don't hold your people back just because you don't have the confidence you can keep them as they grow and succeed. Which leads me to my last point…

WHEN THE FRUIT IS RIPE, PICK IT.

When your people are ready to advance, make it happen. Don't fall into the trap of waiting until they have another job offer to let them know how important they are. Once you have a trained thoroughbred, you had better get it on a track and let it start running; thoroughbreds are not meant to be kept in a stable until you are out of all the other horses and need a replacement. Cut them loose, and let them do what they have been training to do. We often lose very good employees because other people see more value in them than we do. Use 'em or lose 'em!

One of the clear business objectives of any organization should be helping the people in it grow and expand their capabilities. This will not happen by accident, so make sure you are putting the time, effort, and focus into helping your people get better. Doing so will pay many times over. Great leaders have great folks around them and are proud of it!

A Quest for Fire

S O, BY NOW YOU MAY BE THINKING, "Great people hire other great people. Do that enough, and pretty soon your organization is made up of great people from top to bottom. Right?"

Not hardly. I have yet to meet an organization with truly great people from top to bottom. I would challenge anyone who has been in business very long who says they know of such an organization, because I am not sure it is financially realistic to hire the best in every position in your organization. Notice I said "hire."

When we spend all of our time coveting people who are high achievers at other places, especially at our competition, we are very often chasing smoke, when in fact, what we need to go after is fire. Once we see smoke, the action has already happened. By then, the heat is gone, and all we have left is the aftermath of energy.

So, with that picture in mind, how do we avoid the myth of chasing smoke, of chasing talent that may or may not perform for us and that we may or may not be able to afford? The answer is not an easy one. But we can look at a few clues to help us in our quest for fire.

HISTORY DOES NOT ALWAYS PORTEND THE FUTURE.

Salespeople who have succeeded in one company often fail to live up to expectations when they change companies, especially if it involves a pledge to "bring business with them." Even if they truly were successful in their previous position, there is no guarantee that they will automatically succeed in your operation. We all can be tempted to hire away our competitor's top producer (for whatever reasons). But if you insist on doing that, pay for performance, not for potential. High achievers, especially in the sales arena, almost always react better to the tradeoff of a lower weekly or monthly guarantee in exchange for significant earnings potential for exceeding realistic expectations. You will be able to rest better at night when you have a compensation package that shares in the fruits of success (sharing in the profits, especially those beyond expectations) instead of rewarding mediocrity based on past performance.

KNOW WHAT IS NEEDED IN EACH POSITION.

Michael Gerber, author of the bestseller *The E Myth Revisited: Why Most Small Businesses Don't Work and What To Do About It*, says your goal should be to hire people with the lowest possible skill set for a particular position. That's right, the lowest. His idea is to then design a system around those people and supplement them with a few key high achievers scattered in particular positions. His premise is that you simply can't afford to have the best at every position. If you are running an airline, as his theory goes, you don't need "great" pilots. You need technically proficient pilots with a very strong safety and maintenance system around them and strong leadership. Airlines just can't afford to pay to have great pilots in every cockpit. They need to be good, but they don't necessarily need to be great. Think about how this might apply to your business.

GROW YOUR OWN.

An idea closely related to the first clue above is that you have a much better chance of knowing what you have when you grow your own talent. And to be effective, you have to understand that every employee is not destined for greatness. Part of the challenge is to identify those within your organization who have potential and groom them and train them accordingly. Too many companies spend time trying to put lipstick on a pig, when all they really need was a plain old pig. Some pigs are just not meant to wear lipstick. The key is to know who is who and then put your effort into those with potential.

Every company should have a "farm team" (no pun intended) of bench talent they are constantly developing to one day play in the big leagues. If you don't have that farm team, you are putting your company's future at risk.

Great teams are very seldom full of superstars. In fact, too many superstars on a team usually results in a meltdown of some kind from time to time (see the LA Lakers, New York Yankees, and the U.S. Ryder Cup golf teams of the past decade). Not only is the chemistry tough to make work, total payroll almost always becomes too high a hurdle to overcome. In fact, when the Florida Marlins won the World Series a few years ago, the team was immediately dismantled to save money.

In business, we can't afford to ramp up to win the World Series just one time; we have to have a team that can win every year, and that takes a little bit of everything when it comes to employees.

IN BUSINESS, WE CAN'T AFFORD TO RAMP UP TO
WIN THE WORLD SERIES JUST ONE TIME; WE HAVE
TO HAVE A TEAM THAT CAN WIN EVERY YEAR

Yes, it would be nice to have an office full of great, and I mean great employees. It's just not totally realistic. Sometimes what we need is "good" people working in a "great" system. If you can work to achieve both of these goals, good people and a great system, you have a far better opportunity for long-term success in your organization.

Great leaders know *what*, and very often *who*, is needed to achieve the vision—the preferred outcome. By truly understanding your organization's needs and searching for the people who fit those needs, you have a better chance of finding that "fire" you are after instead of just chasing the elusive, and ultimately useless, smoke.

Getting Off on the Right Foot

ONCE YOU HAVE QUALITY PEOPLE in place, the real challenge has just begun. How do you effectively bring new employees into your company? What kind of orientation and training do they receive in their very important first days on the job? How are they integrated into the current workforce? While some companies have fairly sophisticated processes to address these issues, many companies "play it by ear," depending on the employee, and some companies absolutely fly by the seat of their pants. In these cases, the employee and the company usually suffer.

It is important for a new employee to fully grasp a number of areas. However, two of these can very well make or break the new team member. They include the following:

1) Ensure that everyone understands the new employee's job description and duties, and;

2) Ensure that the new employee clearly understands the basic guiding principles by which your company operates. In other words, what does your company stand for?

By clearly understanding these two areas, any new team member will become a more valuable, and happier, part of your company from day one. But why? What is it about these two issues that make them so important? Let's take an in-depth look at each one.

It is important for all employees to have a firm grasp of their job description. In fact, every person in your company should have a job description; if they do not, get it done in the next thirty days. There is no excuse not to. But new employees often are not exactly sure what to expect in the new job. It is a new work environment. They have new people around them, and they are coming into a new job with some level of trepidation.

In addition, the rest of your employees may be just as much in the dark. Why was the new person hired? How much is he being paid? Is it more than me? Is he after my job? None of these questions may be justifiable. However, anything on the minds of your people is valid and must be dealt with. This can be accomplished by making sure everyone knows and understands the role and function of any new employee.

WHY WAS THE NEW PERSON HIRED?
HOW MUCH IS HE BEING PAID?

Regardless of what process you use for new employee orientation, it should include a discussion about company values. These values can serve to provide moral boundaries for the employee to use in the decision-making process, and the values are difficult to absorb casually. Sometimes, when they are obtained by what I call "corporate osmosis," they are not clear, making them open to personal interpretation.

Someone, ideally the owner or one of the top leaders in the company, should personally communicate these values to new employees. And don't make them clichés; make them real. For instance:

- We do not break the law to meet customer demands.

- We value openness and communication, and you will be evaluated on both.

- We believe we win as a team, and we expect you to work as a team. We all have specific job functions, but you are expected to pitch in when needed in other areas.

Information this important should not to be left to happenstance or interpretation. Communicate clearly from day one what you expect, and you are much more likely to get what you expect.

What a new employee learns early, regardless of whether it is right or wrong, becomes standard operating procedure. It is much easier to impact the thought process of new employees in the beginning than to try to change their attitude and actions later. Whether we're talking about a custodian or a vice president, clear expectations and communication from day one make life better for all parties involved. As a leader, it is critical that you look at your orientation process immediately and make sure it is being done effectively—for everyone's sake.

Does Your Team Have a Playbook?

MANY PEOPLE BELIEVE FOOTBALL is a combination of athletic talent and brute force. But the truth is, especially at the professional level, players have to have a thorough understanding of the game and a very deep knowledge of their individual position. In addition, they have to literally memorize dozens of pages of specific information from the team's playbook. What to do, when to do it, and where to be when they do it.

This all comes while the players spend hundreds of hours a year reviewing videotape—both of their own team and of the opponent's team. Then each week, new plays are added in an attempt to stay one step ahead of the competition. The playbook, a three-ring binder for most teams, literally gets thicker as the year goes on.

Without that playbook, without that basic understanding and continuous learning, football would be a bunch of talented and committed players all running around doing their own thing. Every now and then, due to pure talent, a player might accidentally wind up in the right place at the right time and have some success. But how much better is the team by all working off the same playbook?

Business is really no different. What does your company's playbook look like? Are your employees all playing off the same set of plays? Do they all understand your company's basic values? Do they know where they should be on every play in relation to the rest of the team? Are you continuously reviewing game films to know what everyone is doing right and wrong? And are you consistently adding new plays to the playbook in order to stay one step ahead of the competition?

We can learn a great deal from the way football teams prepare.

ARE YOUR EMPLOYEES ALL PLAYING
OFF THE SAME SET OF PLAYS?

PREPARING RIGHT FROM DAY ONE.

When football players report at the beginning of the year, they spend time reviewing the basics: blocking, tackling, conditioning. It is critical to get off on the right foot. So it is with our business. It is important that all employees go through some kind of initial orientation in which they learn the basics about the company. What do we stand for? Why do we do what we do? What are the expectations? So often, new people in our company don't get the advantage of starting off from square one; they get forced into the daily grind before we have the chance to really provide them the foundation, and the information, they need to get off on the right foot. Those first few days are critical. Take advantage of them.

DEVELOPING A COMPREHENSIVE PLAYBOOK.

All great teams need a playbook—especially in business. Notice I didn't say "policy manual." What I'm talking about is a tool your people can use when it comes time to make decisions. The playbook could contain a number of items, including the following:

- Mission statement, goals, and objectives;

- List of key departments and people in the company;

- List of key customers;

- Message from the owner or other top management;

- List of most frequently asked questions about human resource issues;

- History of the company, etc.

IMPROVING SKILLS EACH WEEK.

What makes sports, especially football, unique is that the participants are constantly learning and, ultimately, improving each week. Our businesses should be no different. We should have a process in place so that our employees have the opportunity to learn and grow, both personally and professionally, on a regular basis. Your employees, with the right support, should be smarter and more effective today than they were a year ago. If not, your team is not growing. If your company does not have a training department, or at least someone responsible for training, you are missing the boat. Great companies are made up of great people who get better at what they do nearly every day. That process doesn't happen accidentally. It should be an objective of every organization, just like profitability and on-time delivery.

COACH INSTEAD OF MANAGE.

Adults do not react well to being told what to do. They do, however, respond very well to encouragement, knowledge transfer, and support. In short, we need more coaches in our business. Not more managers. Spend some time thinking about your leadership team as coaches and how that can promote the kind of win/win relations we need in order to be successful.

Leading a sports team is not that different from leading a business organization. Great coaches, just like great leaders, surround themselves with talented people. They continually grade and reward effort, as well as results, in order to make sure the best people are on the field at all times. And finally, coaches and leaders both understand that they can't win the game on their own. By providing a vision of where the team needs to go, coaches and leaders alike lay out a roadmap for success and then provide the tools to help the team achieve positive results.

Sports and business are very much alike. They both need a combination of talent and coordination so that the team can reach its highest potential. And they both need a playbook so that everyone can be in the right place at the right time. Without it, you can end up with great effort but unsatisfactory results. Remember: effort alone doesn't make for a winning team.

Bringing the Whole Team into the Huddle

I T IS NOT UNUSUAL FOR ORGANIZATIONS to bring together their management team from time to time, often on an annual basis, to develop overall company objectives. These objectives can vary greatly from company to company. They can range from revenue and profit objectives to decreasing employee absenteeism and most everything in between. And these objectives usually make very good sense for the organization. Unfortunately, sometimes they are never met.

REALISTIC OBJECTIVES ARE OFTEN NOT MET
BECAUSE THE PEOPLE MOST RESPONSIBLE FOR
MEETING THEM ARE NOT PROPERLY BROUGHT
INTO THE MIX UNTIL IT IS TOO LATE.

Is the failure to reach these goals and objectives because they are poorly thought out or ill-conceived? Is it because the goals are unrealistic or even wishful thinking? Sure, all of these answers are possible. However, realistic objectives are often not met because the people most responsible for meeting them are not properly brought into the mix until it is too late.

Often, the process goes something like this: Senior management comes together for a planning session or budget meeting. From this session comes a series of objectives, some company-oriented and others department-related.

Each manager is assigned his or her role in meeting the objectives and, hopefully, a strategy emerges wherein each department determines its role in helping achieve the objectives. Unfortunately, the planning process often stops right there, and thus, the challenge begins.

Upper management often informs rank-and-file employees of departmental and company goals and objectives by meeting or memo. The employees are given a timeframe for achieving the goals and regular updates on where they stand versus where they need to be. Unfortunately, the true rank-and-file employee never understands or buys into his or her individual role in achieving success as defined by upper management.

One very useful tool in bringing every member of the team into the huddle and getting buy-in on goals and objectives is to involve them in setting the goals and objectives. When employees are involved in charting their own path, they very often are more aggressive and, certainly, more realistic in striving for improvement. Management can always have veto, or edit, authority over any goals employees set for themselves.

But regardless of who sets the goals and objectives, the most effective tool is to let individual employees tell management what roll they will play in meeting targets. Instead of issuing orders from the top, ask for buy-in from the bottom. It is only human nature that we are more likely to make the extra effort to carry out our own ideas. In addition, individuals may very well know better than management how to best meet the objectives.

So, the next time you come up with annual goals or objectives, communicate them to every employee and every associate, and then take the extra step of asking them what three specific strategies they will initiate to help move the organization to and beyond these benchmarks. Every single employee. Every single associate. You may need to meet with some one-on-one to help them understand their respective roles in the process, and you may even have to help them develop their own strategies. But I can promise you the time will be well spent, and the process will likely be informative and helpful for both of you.

We generally get from our people what we expect from them. When we raise our expectations, we often are rewarded with improved results. When we give them the opportunity to chart their own future, they are more likely to reach the destination. If you allow your people to tell you themselves how they will meet the goals and objectives, you will get an organization full of people who know what has to happen in order for the organization to succeed.

With this strategy, you truly are leading your people by doing the following:

1)   Providing the preferred outcome;

2)   Allowing them to chart their own course to success; and

3)   Getting out of their way and letting them do their jobs.

When you surround yourself with the right people, they are uniquely qualified to provide their own direction, and you will be much more likely to reach the goals and objectives needed to advance your organization.

Spreading Your Expectations to Achieve the Best from Everyone

HERE IS ANOTHER VERSION OF THE 80/20 RULE. You may know this one. It says that 80 percent of your business comes from 20 percent of your customers, that 80 percent of your problems come from 20 percent of your customers, and so on. This theory seems to apply in many areas of our businesses and personal lives.

Another area to which the rule applies, if not literally then at least figuratively, is in the area of employee productivity. Pat Croce, former owner of the Philadelphia 76ers and now a noted business author, says his business experience shows that 80 percent of the results comes from 20 percent of his employees. These are his "go-to" people. We all have them. They are the folks we turn to when something has to get done, when good is not good enough and it has to be great, when we want to be sure it gets done right.

Using a sports analogy, it's like a major league baseball team having a great "closer" in the bullpen. If you follow baseball, you know that these guys often will not pitch more than thirty to forty pitches in a game. They are very seldom called on until the eighth or ninth inning and are expected to "close the door" on opposing batters, hence the name. They are often paid much more than other relievers and even many starting pitchers. Despite the temptation, managers know they can't overuse these precious commodities. They have a very precise role, and, while they could probably excel in any role if given the time, it is critical not to abuse their talent and capabilities.

We all have closers in our business. The problem is, we often don't exercise the same good judgment regarding when we should call on these "closers." In fact, we overuse them. We often call on them too quickly. When we do that, not only does it put undue pressure on them, but it allows the other team members to not pull their own load.

So when we see the 80/20 rule come to life in our business as it relates to employee productivity, it is often the result of our actions as managers and leaders. We are allowing, or causing in some cases, some of our people to excel, while others are allowed to be "Eighty-Percenters." How do we overcome the tendency to go to our "closer" too quickly, and how do we learn to utilize the entire staff effectively? Here are a few tips:

BE PATIENT.

As leaders, we have to set clear expectations and then allow our people time to meet them. We are often too impatient and go to our "closer" before giving our other pitchers the opportunity to excel. Quality takes time; don't go to the bullpen too quickly.

KNOW YOUR TALENT.

Leaders need to understand the talent they have on their team. Some people have a higher gear to kick into, and some don't. If you know that the task at hand will require that higher gear, don't assign the task to an employee without a higher gear to shift to; doing so simply creates a future problem. Have realistic expectations of your people, and then act on what you know.

DON'T BE AFRAID TO MAKE A TRADE.

If you have employees who consistently under-perform, don't keep sending them to the mound. It is not fair to them or to the others in your organization. Make a trade, or cut them from the team. It is easy to justify keeping someone because of a specific talent—and often it is the right thing to do. But sometimes we are blind to what others see. When you make sure you are making a fair and objective judgment about the value of individual team members, you are more likely to make the right judgment.

LET THE PLAYERS PLAY.

I am a firm believer that we often don't allow our people to perform to their level of capability. Many situations will work themselves out, and the people involved will meet our expectations, if we simply allow it to happen. Make sure you and your processes allow your employees the opportunity to succeed. Provide the vision for your people, and then give them the time and tools to achieve it.

THE 80/20 RULE DOESN'T HAVE TO APPLY TO EMPLOYEE EFFECTIVENESS

When we understand the power of our own decisions, we will better understand the value of what our people can do for us. Don't be the one to make Pat Croce's experience come to life in your business. The 80/20 rule doesn't have to apply to employee effectiveness; it only will when we allow it.

Establishing Policies That Empower

TODAY'S MOST EFFECTIVE AND EFFICIENT businesses are moving towards policies that are more empowering and less restrictive. In other words, these companies develop and implement policies that help their workers understand what they can and should do, rather than policies that just that tell the employees what they shouldn't and can't do. The difference is subtle in language but substantial in impact.

A local utility company, working to significantly enhance the effectiveness of its employees, found that its policies and procedures were very rigid and restrictive and were ultimately causing more problems than they prevented. After a period of continually addressing and tweaking policies, the company finally settled on an attendance policy and dress code that literally reads, "Come to work and wear clothes." While this may take the concept of flexibility to an extreme, it does point out how companies are trying to use policies and procedures not to control employees but instead to free them to do their jobs.

Following are a few suggestions to consider when drafting the "rules" your employees operate under:

1) Every time you establish a new procedure, go back and see if you can eliminate an old one.

2) Be careful not to establish a new policy or procedure in reaction to a specific incident.

3) Make sure your policies and procedures are consistent with your company philosophy. Don't talk about having a "family atmosphere" and then tell people they are not allowed to take personal calls. Neither of these policies is unrealistic on its own, but the two simply don't jive with each other. Great leaders are consistent with their words and their actions.

4) Make sure your policies and procedures ultimately promote the goal of serving the customer. Often, our rules inhibit our ability to meet customer needs. This goes back to the concept of making sure our rules are instructive and empowering instead of restrictive and punitive.

MAKE SURE YOUR POLICIES AND
PROCEDURES ULTIMATELY PROMOTE
THE GOAL OF SERVING THE CUSTOMER.

---

5) Understand the impact of your policies and procedures before you make them public. I have written about the "emotional wake" left by your decisions. By working through the organizational impact of a new policy on paper, you have a much better opportunity to enhance your people's effectiveness instead of limiting it.

AT&T eliminated most of its company travel policies in favor of an elegantly simple corporate travel statement: "Use your good judgment, always keeping the shareholder in mind." While this "rule" leaves room for a great deal of interpretation and abuse, AT&T believes it is hiring the kind of people who will understand the policy and make it work for the organization.

Do you have the right policies and procedures for your people? Do you have the right people for your policies and procedures? I would go so far as to say that if you have a policy or procedure in place that started because of one employee, that rule should go away—and so should the person you created it for.

Now would be a great time to review your company handbook and make sure the criteria your people operate under are current, applicable, instructive, and empowering. By doing so, you are truly providing your employees what they need to achieve the preferred vision.

Meetings That Matter

GREAT GOLFERS ARE KNOWN for their ability to play well on and around the greens. In fact, most golf instructors will tell you that the quickest way to score better in golf is to practice your short game. When you have the urge to go to the driving range with visions of hitting 330-yard Tiger Woods drives, you really should be on the practice green working on how to hit that flop shot from just off the green or practicing six-foot putts.

The reason is simple: over half the shots you hit in a typical round of golf happen around or on the green. So the best opportunity to lower your score comes by working on the area of your game that has the most impact on your score. And that is your short game.

In business, we have a similar situation when it comes to meetings. Research says the average businessperson in America spends nearly a third of his or her time in meetings of some sort. And on top of that, nearly 70 percent of people surveyed indicated they felt that some of the time they spend in meetings is unproductive or wasted. Yet, how much time do we spend learning how to conduct more effective and efficient meetings? Not much.

I am convinced we could immediately impact productivity in our organizations if we conducted better meetings. If our meetings were better, our people would be more engaged in the meetings, we would get more done during the meetings, and people would leave with a greater sense of accomplishment. With the shift to a team concept over the past decade, the importance of great meetings has become even more crucial. The more people involved in a meeting, the more collective time is wasted if the meeting is not productive.

As a leader, how much thought and effort do you put into meetings you conduct or are a part of? Are you doing the best job you can to make sure the meeting is productive? Are you fulfilling your role as a leader when it comes to utilizing your people's time and talents? Following are a few key points to consider before you call your next meeting.

WHY ARE WE MEETING?

And the answer shouldn't be, "Because it's Monday morning, and we always meet on Monday morning." Standing meetings do more to waste time and frustrate workers than any other type of meeting. And often when there is a good reason to meet, the reason is not communicated prior to the meeting, so workers walk in unsure of why they have been summoned and unprepared to provide meaningful input. Make sure everyone knows the purpose of the meeting—ahead of time. Even if it is a standing meeting—daily, weekly, or monthly—remind all those involved of the purpose of the meeting.

FOCUS ON THE RIGHT ISSUES.

We don't meet because we have issues; we meet because we want solutions. It doesn't matter the purpose of the meeting, whether it's an update or a strategic planning meeting, the goal should be to walk out of the meeting with answers. Too many meetings waste time focusing on the problem, whom to blame, and what we have tried before to fix it. Identify the issue at the very beginning of the meeting, make sure the focus stays on the issue at hand, and ask, before the meeting concludes, if the issue was addressed. It is not uncommon for meetings to get sidetracked and get completely off the subject at hand. Don't let it happen.

INVOLVE THE RIGHT PEOPLE.

It is vital that the right people are in the meeting to address the issues being discussed. It sounds simple, but we often make this mistake. Even if it means bringing someone in after the meeting starts, the people who are empowered to address the issue being discussed should be around the table. On the other hand, don't require people to attend meetings that don't pertain to them. It may mean a little more work for you as a leader to make sure this happens, but it is well worth the time. It is often easier to summon all the department heads to the conference room for a typical meeting. But the truth is, your department heads are busy, and if they don't need to be in that meeting, they shouldn't be there. Take the time to determine, every time, who really needs to be in the meeting, and involve only those who are truly needed to address the issues at hand.

HAVE FEWER MEETINGS.

As leaders, we often use meetings as a crutch, because we don't always do a good job of communicating one-on-one with our direct reports. Because we are not sure what everyone is up to, we call a meeting to receive a report from the team. For instance, you've been gone for a week and, upon returning, call a meeting to find out generally where things are. These meetings go on all the time and are very frustrating to everyone but the person who called the meeting. Keep in mind that your employees have to stop doing what you are paying them to do in order to come and tell you what they are doing. By the way, when you call this kind of meeting, you are not leading. You are managing. As I've said, your thoroughbreds can't run if you don't have them on the track. Meeting rooms are the horse stalls of American business. Let your horses run; don't keep them tied up with meetings that aren't completely necessary.

YOUR THOROUGHBREDS CAN'T RUN IF YOU DON'T
HAVE THEM ON THE TRACK. MEETING ROOMS ARE
THE HORSE STALLS OF AMERICAN BUSINESS.

JUSTIFY EVERY MEETING.

Finally, make an effort to justify every meeting held in your organization. If it doesn't need to happen, don't have it. It doesn't matter if you have had a Monday morning staff meeting every Monday for twenty years—get up next Monday morning and determine if you really need to have that meeting that day. It takes effort on your part but will absolutely help your people, and ultimately your organization, operate more efficiently and effectively. It is also important to remember that your people are watching you to decide how to act. So, if you call or conduct ineffective meetings, you are giving your people permission to do the same.

Great leaders take the time to pay attention to what matters. When you focus on how to best use the time and talents of your people, you are truly focusing on what matters most. Make it a priority to have better meetings. And the next time you have the urge to call a meeting because you feel out of the loop—don't. When you communicate better with your people every day, you'll find less need to call meetings. That will make you a better leader and will give your thoroughbreds the time and room they need to run.

Building Ownership in Your Organization

IN MY LEADERSHIP SESSIONS, I ASK ATTENDEES how many of them have washed a rental car before returning it. While every now and then one or two people will raise their hand to say they did indeed wash the vehicle, for a variety of reasons, before returning it, the vast majority say they never have. When I ask why, the answer is consistently, and logically, "Because I don't own that vehicle. That's the rental car folks' problem."

I believe you can fairly conclude from my ongoing unofficial rental car research that people have a tendency to take better care of something in which they have ownership. I believe the same applies to our organizations. When our employees believe the company is "theirs," they tend to take better care of it and its customers.

WHEN OUR EMPLOYEES BELIEVE THE
COMPANY IS "THEIRS," THEY TEND TO TAKE
BETTER CARE OF IT AND ITS CUSTOMERS.

If I've heard it once, I've heard it dozens of times from company owners and top managers: "How do I get my people to care about this company as much as I do?" The answer is to create the same sense of ownership in your employees that you approach your own business with on a daily basis. So, how do we create this kind of ownership in our organizations without giving up the equity we have worked so hard to develop?

Following are a number of strategies successful companies are using to create a sense of ownership throughout the organization.

BEGIN WITH A CHANGE IN YOUR ATTITUDE.

You can't just put up a poster, put out a memo, and tell people they should start acting like owners. You, and your senior managers, have to believe in the concept and begin to treat your employees as you would those who truly have an equity stake in the operation.

SHARE INFORMATION WITH EMPLOYEES AS THOUGH THEY ARE OWNERS.

Employees are best able to deal with your business when they know the facts about your—and their—business. Be willing to share financial information, especially that information that pertains directly to their responsibilities, in a timely and consistent manner, not just when it's convenient or serves your purpose. Give your people the information they need to manage your business like it's their business.

HOLD EMPLOYEES ACCOUNTABLE LIKE OWNERS.

If your company suffers financially, you suffer. If it thrives financially, you likely thrive. Extend the concept to your employees. Make sure they understand that owners have ultimate accountability, and hold them to it. Because they have a greater upside, they should be held to a higher standard. You have to provide an atmosphere in which your employees take it personally when something doesn't go as planned—not one that allows them to say, "Hey, I just work here. That's somebody else's problem."

COMPENSATE EMPLOYEES LIKE OWNERS.

By this I mean that there should be some incentive for the overall company to perform above expectations. Some call it profit-sharing. I prefer to call it results-sharing. Many companies reward employees when expectations are exceeded but don't follow the same standard when expectations are not met (see item 3), but true ownership means that employees must share in the agony as well as the ecstasy. You have to apply this with some common sense, but you must make sure the compensation program reflects overall company results, not just profits.

GET OUT OF THE WAY OF YOUR EMPLOYEES.

Once you have begun to create an atmosphere of ownership among your employees, let them do what you have hired them to do. They are not going to feel like owners if they are micro-managed by you or your immediate reports. You can't call people owners and then walk around telling them what they can and can't do all day.

HAVE OWNER TYPES IN YOUR ORGANIZATION.

All people are not made to be owners. Creating a sense of ownership often requires a review of your staff to make sure you have the right people in your organization. As I said earlier, you can't expect to just send a memo and have everyone change their attitudes. This process takes time, it takes consistency, and it takes the right people. This can be a great opportunity to systematically review your ranks and understand better who you have working for you and what makes them tick.

Obviously, every company is not going to take this concept and run with it fully. However, the best companies in the world are those that have created a sense of ownership among their employees, and any of these strategies you can employ in your organization will help.

When you can go to bed at night and believe your employees care as much about your business as you do, you have created an environment that is almost guaranteed to be better for you, your employees, and your customers. Remember, you get out of your people what you expect of them. Expect them to act like owners, treat them like owners, and provide them the tools owners need—and your rental car will never be returned unwashed again. OK, maybe that's stretching it a little.

Around the Campfire

KEEP COMMUNICATION FLOWING FREELY

THE SINGLE BIGGEST PROBLEM IN
COMMUNICATION IS THE ILLUSION
THAT IT HAS TAKEN PLACE.

GEORGE BERNARD SHAW

Getting Your Message Across When It Matters Most

ONE OF THE COMMON TRAITS of great leaders is their ability to communicate effectively. After all, by definition, a leader provides a vision for the future that makes others want to achieve that vision. If a leader can't project the desired outcome through effective communication, then leadership never really occurs.

That being said, I believe a significant amount of the problems we have in business today are due to a lack of communication. That failure to communicate can manifest itself in a number of ways:

- Not making clear the goal or objective (If you don't know where you're going, how can you know when you've arrived?);

- Not communicating clear expectations (If people don't receive feedback, how can they know if they are on the right track?);

- Not providing supportive communication to those involved in the process (How can people know you are pleased or displeased with them if you don't let them know?);

- Providing useless communication when meaningful communication is needed (What you focus on is what your people will focus on. Make sure you are managing what matters).

Now, don't get me wrong. You don't have to be able to stand up and make a rip-roaring, bring-the-house-down speech in order to be a great communicator. Granted, it doesn't hurt to have that ability. However, what makes a leader great is simply understanding the need for effective and consistent communication. My former boss, a leader from whom I learned a great deal, didn't say much. But when he finally did talk, you knew you had better listen, because it was going to be important. In that way, he was a great communicator.

KNOW THAT NEARLY EVERYTHING
YOU DO SENDS A MESSAGE, WHETHER
YOU MEAN FOR IT TO OR NOT.

The first and most important step to becoming an exceptional leader is to simply understand the power of what you communicate and how you communicate it. As a leader, people are looking to you each day to see how you handle situations and people. What you do or say sets the standard, good or bad. So, to get the process started, know that nearly everything you do sends a message, whether you mean for it to or not.

There are dozens of examples, such as:

- What hours do you work?

- What do you wear?

- How do you treat others?

- Do you have a positive attitude?

- Are you consistent in your actions?

- Do you take time for those around you?

How you answer these questions will decide how you "preach when you don't even realize you are in the pulpit." Great leaders know they communicate almost constantly—and not just when they deliver a speech, write a memo, or make a presentation. Great leaders know that communication is a twenty-four-hour-a-day process and not just a task on your to-do list.

One of my favorite admonitions to leaders is "Don't let your actions speak louder than your memos." For instance, don't talk about the importance of safety and then sit by and let operations force a driver into a potentially unsafe situation in the name of productivity. Don't talk about the importance of honesty and then fudge on your expense report or allow your best salesperson to fudge on hers because she exceeds sales goals each month. Remember, your actions must be consistent with your words, or the message will be fuzzy or even get completely lost.

When it appears that your people may not be "getting it," and the results just aren't there, don't blame them. More times than not, it is because "it" isn't clear to them. Start with yourself, be clear about the message you are sending, and make sure the message is consistent with company goals and objectives. After all, it's not the message sent that matters; it's the message received that counts. Great leaders understand the power of communication and their role in the process.

What You Haven't Said
May Come Back to Bite You

OVER EASTER WEEKEND a few years ago, my son Clayton, then four, got our attention when he emerged from a room at Jill's parents' house with a pair of scissors in his hand and a very creative, self-administered haircut. He looked like he had experienced a head-on crash with a Weed Eater.

Trying very hard not to laugh and to maintain the stern demeanor of a concerned parent, I asked him why he had done it. His answer was, "Because I needed it." In typical, not-thinking-before-you-speak fashion, I said, "Clayton, you're not supposed to cut your own hair." And in very typical four-year-old fashion, he answered, "Daddy, you never said not to."

Wow! That will get your attention. That phrase immediately throws you into a mental inventory of what else you haven't told your young children not to do. When you think about it, that is a very logical response. Sure, children figure out on their own not to do things that will hurt them. Sometimes, they learn the hard way. But what about those things with no obvious negative consequences, other than the need to wear a hat throughout Easter Day? What seems so obvious to us as parents, or leaders, may not be so obvious to those we parent or lead.

As we continue to talk about the issue of effective communication as a leadership tool, it is vital that we look at our business and take that same mental inventory of what we have *not* told our people. What information have we withheld, either because we didn't think our employees particularly needed to know or because we just never got around to sharing it? The fact is, our employees and associates cannot deal with information they don't have. They can't respond to a situation they don't know about. They simply cannot meet expectations they are not aware of.

Things happen in our business every day that our people need to know about. Some management experts go as far as advocating sharing all financial information with all employees in order to give them the information they need to help the company be profitable. There is debate over the effectiveness of that method, although many companies have achieved great financial results using the concept. In fact, those same companies are very enlightened and likely would achieve some level of success whether they shared financial information with all employees or not.

That being said, I believe companies need to do a much better job of sharing company information. What kind of information? The information employees need to take care of your business, including but not limited to the following:

- Financial information, such as the key indicators used by ownership to determine fiscal health; and

- Key information on key customers so employees can deal with each in a unique and effective manner. For instance, information that a key customer is in the middle of renegotiating its business relationships, including the one with your company.

YOU CAN'T JUST WRITE OUT A MEMO
ONE DAY THAT INCLUDES EVERYTHING
YOU'VE NEVER SHARED WITH FOLKS.

While all this information may be obvious to you and your top managers, many employees don't understand why the company does what it does, so sharing that information can be very valuable. How do you accomplish that? You can't just write out a memo one day that includes everything you've never shared with folks.

One very effective way is through a company publication in a "Did you know?" format. For instance, you might address a vehicle life cycle issue by saying, "Did you know that by trading our trucks every three years, we are able to reduce our maintenance costs by X number of dollars? In turn, our equipment is much more dependable, and we have fewer lost revenue days because of unusable equipment. In fact, since we have adopted this policy, we have increased our profit to the bottom line by X dollars."

Again, this information is not heart-stopping in substance and is obviously not news to you and some others. However, helping the average employee better understand why the company does what it does will empower that employee to make unsupervised decisions (let's face it, they happen every day) with a better understanding of the company's goals and objectives.

So the next time one of your employees walks into your office with scissors in his hands (metaphorically speaking) and a bad haircut, before you ask the question, "Why did you do that?" make sure you have been communicating effectively whatever information the employee needs to make the right decisions on your behalf. Be willing, as a leader, to share important information, both good and bad. Knowledge and information equal power, so you should provide your people with the power they need to take care of your business and your customers.

You Are Who You Are...
Regardless of Where You Are

EVER HAD A VERY tough day at work? It seemed that everybody in the company came by to talk. You stared down one crisis after another. You used your management skills to put out several raging fires, and you used your leadership prowess to prevent another two. You were an exceptional communicator in all cases. You were on! But wow, are you ever talked out!

Now it's time to go home. When you arrive, your spouse wants to know how the day went. Did anything interesting happen? Did Bob show up for work? Did you get that new customer and new contract? Did you pick up the dry cleaning? Are you going out of town this week? Can you take the kids to that birthday party Saturday morning?

Innocent questions in most cases. Idle conversation? Perhaps. The only problem is, after the kind of day you've had, idle conversation is not particularly high on your evening agenda.

Sound familiar? Many of us go through this scenario in some form or another every now and then. Some of us more than others—you know who you are. The fact is, effective communication is not an issue that should be handled differently at work and at home. Great leaders are great communicators...wherever they are and whatever they are doing. The real challenge is to not let what happens at home negatively impact your work and, most importantly, to not let what happens at work negatively impact your life at home. Often, effective and consistent communication, especially at home, is the only way to avoid what I like to call, and not so delicately I might add, *conversational constipation.*

EFFECTIVE COMMUNICATION IS NOT
AN ISSUE THAT SHOULD BE HANDLED
DIFFERENTLY AT WORK AND AT HOME.

In the book *Fierce Conversations—Achieving Success at Work & in Life, One Conversation at a Time,* Dr. Susan Scott says we must all discard the notion that we respond differently depending on who we are with and what the situation is. It is simply not true that we deal with our family differently than we do our employees, that we deal with customers differently than we do our family, and that we deal with our friends differently than we do strangers.

Dr. Scott says that when you squeeze an orange you get orange juice – whether you are at work or at home. You never get tomato juice or apple juice. The same is true for each of us. When things are tense or we are under pressure, in our personal lives or in our careers, we can't hide it in a closet. It comes to work with us; it comes home with us. You are who you are, everywhere you go.

Enlightened leaders come to understand the incredibly self-healing properties of communication and, more specifically, conversation. They know the value comes in letting conversation happen at just the time it seems most comfortable to shut down. You simply cannot turn on and turn off your communication skills. Why? Because that one person in front of whom you clam up that may well be the one who needs the conversation most. And that can happen at work, at home, at church…you pick the place, and it's possible.

Just imagine the firefighter who spends all day putting out fires. Then, at the end of the day at home, he finds his house on fire and decides he has fought enough fires that day. He doesn't have that luxury, and neither do we—as leaders.

So the next time you feel the need to turn off the communication switch, understand the potential impact, both to you and others. Understand they have not been there for all of your conversations all day long; they are simply asking for one opportunity to converse. In fact, they may be asking for their only opportunity to converse. Leaders understand the impact their actions have on others.

But perhaps more importantly, leaders who are truly in touch with their role understand their own personal need for communication. They clearly see the value in sharing information with others and the feedback that comes from that exchange. And perhaps most importantly, they fully understand that the time it seems most appropriate to clam up is often the best time to open up.

So the next time you are worn out, talked out, or burned out, understand that communication is always a valuable tool. It works in good times and bad. It is effective whether you are at work or at home. When you have a difficult decision to make and the voices are bouncing through your head, take that as a sign that you ought to be talking to someone else. It is during difficult times and when facing tough decisions that we often suffer from what I described as *conversational constipation* and withdraw, when, in fact, we should be reaching out to communicate, to converse.

Leaders are great communicators at home and at work, day and night, in good times and bad, when they have to and when they don't and, most importantly, when they want to and when they don't.

Start with the Basics When Developing a Roadmap

WHEN CARTOGRAPHERS START the process of laying out a state map, they begin with the basics. These basics include the major cities, the borders, the capitol city, and major landmarks such as mountain peaks, interstate and U.S. highways, etc. With these basics on the map, it is then time to start filling in the details, such as smaller cities and towns, state and county roads, and state parks. Without the basics, the detail does little good.

For instance, in my home state of Texas, no one ever describes Waco as being ten miles from the intersection of Highways 34 and 21. Instead, people say, "Waco is an hour and a half south of Dallas." You never hear anyone say, "Waco is twenty miles from Robinson;" it is two hours north of Austin. We have to have major landmarks, the basics, to know where we are when we travel. The same goes for our business.

We often spend hours developing strategic objectives for our organizations. Increase sales by 8 percent. Reduce billing errors by 50 percent. Increase net profits by 12 percent. We are seldom short on these very specific details about what we expect from our people.

However, what are the basics in our organizational roadmap? What are the major cities, the mountain peaks, and the borders our people need to navigate through business each and every day?

As leaders, we must describe the preferred outcome for our people. And we must describe this outcome in detail. However, we must not forget the basic landmarks that help us define who and what we are. What might our basic objectives look like?

- Treat co-workers, customers. and those around us with integrity and respect;

- Provide the highest levels of service to both our internal and external customers;

- Produce profits for our business.

Many might say these "basics" are obvious. But we must be careful not to take for granted these types of "landmarks." We can cause our people to get so caught up in the destination that we ignore the journey. This promotes an environment in which we reach our objectives, the details, at any cost.

Every company needs specific objectives, specific destinations on the map. But just as well, organizations need the borders within which they must operate. They need to know about the tall mountains they might need to avoid in some situations. They should be aware of the major landmarks to reference in case they become lost on the road to where they are going.

WE CAN'T AFFORD TO GET
SO FOCUSED ON THE DESTINATION
THAT OUR PATH FOR GETTING THERE
BECOMES INCONSEQUENTIAL.

The next time you provide objectives and goals for your organization, make sure you have included a mix of very specific details within the borders of a well-defined roadmap. Don't take for granted that your people get the "big picture." We can't afford to get so focused on the destination that our path for getting there becomes inconsequential.

Great leaders have the gift of vision and the ability to focus on achieving that vision: big-picture awareness with attention to detail. When everyone in our operation can share this mix of vision and focus, we have much better odds of performing at the highest levels of organizational efficiency, service, and profitability.

Goals and Objectives That Work for Everyone

GOALS AND OBJECTIVES that look very promising on paper do little good if they are not embraced by those throughout our organizations. So when our people fail to meet plan—fail to meet our stated expectations—whom do we blame? In most cases, we put the blame everywhere except where it belongs: on ourselves.

Many experts believe that goals and objectives are often not met because the people most responsible for their potential success, the front-line employees, aren't able to clearly understand their roles in obtaining the goals. And while it is easy to blame the receiver for not getting the message, it is imperative that we as the senders do a better job of communicating the message. So the question becomes: how do we leaders do a better job of putting important performance goals in a framework that the people in our organizations can clearly find a handle to grab onto?

Take the very broad objective of improving customer satisfaction. Most every person in any business unit can have a role in improving customer service, whether or not that person deals directly with the customers. Yet, if individual goals and objectives are not specific enough, it becomes easy for some to take the objective for granted and leave it for "them"—whoever "them" is in a particular case.

Following are a few points to help us drive the most important elements of our business plan throughout our organizations.

DRIVE THE TOP LINE TO THE BOTTOM LINE.

Goals and objectives for any organization should tie directly to the bottom line. For instance, as in the example above, improved customer satisfaction is fine, but how does that specifically translate to the bottom line? What performance measurements are specific indicators of success or failure in this area? If you are not able to make that direct connection, your people will not be able to either. Don't lay two dots on the table and expect everyone else to connect them. They may all eventually connect them but take significantly different paths to do so.

DEPARTMENTALIZE AND INDIVIDUALIZE STRATEGIES AND TACTICS.

Goals and objectives are more likely to be achieved when departments and individuals understand their specific roles in achieving them. By taking the extra step of drilling down into an organizational goal to develop properly aligned strategies and tactics, more people are likely to find something they can identify with—or embrace—to help meet plan. When people can clearly see a specific strategy or tactic that applies directly to them, they are more likely to do their part to achieve success—however success is defined.

TIE ORGANIZATIONAL GOALS TO PERFORMANCE REVIEWS.

Once we develop these individualized plans, how do we link them to performance? One very workable method is to tie our goals and objectives in the review process directly to the goals and objectives of the organization. Again using the example above, if our organizational goal is some measurement of greater customer satisfaction, and we have determined the specific role a department or an individual could and should play, then spell these out in an employee's regular performance evaluation. When it is made clear that the employees' evaluation will be based on how they perform against the specific objectives, strategies, and tactics, they are much more likely to focus on them.

When we clearly align, throughout our organization, our goals and objectives, we have a better opportunity for success. When we are able to put in clear language the role each and every person plays in meeting these goals and objectives, we greatly enhance our people's ability to play a meaningful role in the process. As leaders, our role should not be limited to developing strategy and then measuring performance. I can almost assure you that the better job we do in driving this process down throughout our respective organizations, the more likely our people are to embrace their roles in achieving success.

When people can take ownership in a specific strategy because they can identify with it, they are more likely to make it happen. If we, as leaders, don't put it in terms they can grasp, we should look first at ourselves and ask the question: "Were we clear in our expectations?"

WHEN PEOPLE CAN TAKE OWNERSHIP
IN A SPECIFIC STRATEGY BECAUSE THEY
CAN IDENTIFY WITH IT, THEY ARE
MORE LIKELY TO MAKE IT HAPPEN.

Our people will almost always perform up to the expectations we place upon them. By being clear about what is expected, we greatly improve the probability that our employees will reach the goals that we have laid out for them.

The Emotional Wake
of Your Decisions

EVER HAD A DIFFICULT DECISION TO MAKE? I don't mean the kind of decision where the outcome will be hard to implement. I mean the kind of quandary in which the answer is complex, in which there is no obvious "right" thing to do, in which whatever decision you reach has the potential of "unintended consequences."

It is those "unintended consequences" that can cause us serious problems. In fact, enlightened leaders, through their own life experiences, have come to know the importance of understanding the message they are sending with the decisions they make. Unfortunately, the message we intended to send and the one actually received don't always match up. That is when we begin to see the "emotional wake" of our decisions.

As an example, close-knit organizations known for a family-like work environment are often very loyal to their people—sometimes too much so. While the employees in that company may be held to a high standard, they often are given "slack" when problems occur, because that's what we do with our "family." But the truth is, when that leniency goes too far (and it very often does), we mistake loyalty for ignoring the hard choices that come with being in charge. In fact, we convince ourselves we are doing the right thing and that we are "taking care" of our people. But are we really?

Often, we simply don't think about the *emotional wake* of our decisions. Let's look at a particular situation from both sides. We have a long-term employee who is simply not living up to the performance standards required

148

by a new customer. The customer continues to complain, so you decide to retain that employee (because of twenty years of loyalty to the company) but shift those job duties to another person in the department. The thinking, on your part, is that an employee who has given that much effort over a long period should not be penalized simply because one customer has high expectations. You take action you believe sends the message that your company is reasonable and fair and takes care of its employees—the family.

The message that the others in the company possibly receive is different. What they take from the situation is that you are protecting an employee who is not pulling his load, just because he's been employed for a long time. You are allowing him to under-perform, and on top of that you are dumping his work on someone who is performing. With this decision, you have saved an employee but may lose others because of the same decision.

Let's look at it from the other angle. Under the same circumstances, you decide it is not fair to anyone to keep any employee who is not getting the job done; that employee simply must go, regardless of tenure. The message you intend to send is that everyone is treated equally, and everyone has a job to do. The message other employees might receive is that you have no loyalty, that the employee's long-term commitment means nothing, and that customers are clearly more important than the employees of the company, the "family" you say you are so proud of.

ENLIGHTENED LEADERS UNDERSTAND
THE ULTIMATE IMPACT OF THEIR DECISIONS.

Whether the person should be fired or retained is not the lesson here. It is the *emotional wake* of your decisions. What have you left behind once you have pulled the trigger? Is the message you sent the one you truly intended to send?

Enlightened leaders understand the ultimate impact of their decisions. They know that the message they send is not always the message their employees receive. And they fully comprehend the impact of the wake they leave behind.

To be successful in business today, leaders can't simply operate in their own world. In fact, as a leader, our sphere of influence expands significantly as we move up the ladder, and we have to understand the impact our decisions have on those living in that world. It may not mean that the ultimate decision would be different; it could just mean that you think ahead about the implications of that decision and take the appropriate action to deal with any wake you create.

We all make hundreds, if not thousands, of decisions every day. Many, we don't even think about. We must understand the potential wake we leave behind and know that we have a responsibility to those around us to at least consider the ramifications, the message being sent, and the message being received. When we do, we truly are leading our folks instead of managing them.

Nothing Improves Hearing like Praise

DO YOU EVER HAVE THE FEELING some days your communication skills are not what you would like them to be? More to the point, some mornings do you ever feel like you just can't get your point across to your people? Even more bluntly, do you find yourself in situations where your people just don't seem to get it, and your frustrations are rising because you don't seem to be able to help them get it—whatever *it* is?

Communication is a two-way street in every situation. There must be a sender and a receiver in order for effective communication to occur. A short-circuit on either end breaks the cycle. So how do we make sure our people receive the message we send?

> THERE MUST BE A SENDER AND A
> RECEIVER IN ORDER FOR EFFECTIVE
> COMMUNICATION TO OCCUR.

We can't. It's plain and simple: we can't *make* anyone do anything. The only end of the communication equation we can control is our end. To find the answers—and challenges—of how we hold up our end of the communication deal, we only have to look at society to better understand why we don't always make that perfect connection with those around us.

We live in a critical world. It is far easier, and more commonplace, to talk about what is wrong. Take the typical daily newspaper as an example. How long has it been since the lead story on the front page was good news? And it's not just the front page. Look at movie reviews. Sometimes I'm not even sure we see the same version of the movies the reviewers see. They seem to find numerous negatives even in the movies that earn "four stars" or a "thumbs-up." It's almost like these reviewers feel they will lose their jobs if they are too positive.

In our own everyday lives, we often spend so much of our time talking about what's wrong that we don't get around to talking about what's right. Besides, isn't our job to fix problems? It only seems natural that our focus, and therefore much of our communications, would involve "fixing" things and people. The good people don't need us; they're good enough to motivate themselves while we're off solving the problems no one else wants to tackle.

So, it is no wonder that communication can break down. When we leave our offices, when our people see us coming, what are they thinking? Is it, "Uh oh. Here he comes. I wonder what I've done now?" Do our people just assume that if we want to talk to them, something is wrong? It's a little bit like a conversational flinch—you see it coming and just can't help but turn away.

On our worst days, maybe even on a normal day, are we creating this reaction in our people? Do they dread communicating with us, because they know the communication will likely be negative? Hopefully not. But when communication seems to be breaking down, it may very well be because our people are tuning out, since they are expecting bad news. So, how do we begin to improve communication based on what we can control—that is, the message we are delivering?

There is an old adage that says nothing improves a child's hearing like praise. The same goes for adults. If we want to improve communication, we as leaders must balance the bad with the good. We have to make a formal effort to spend time talking to our people about what is right as opposed to just what is wrong. This doesn't mean we have to sugarcoat the problems or even turn our heads away from them. But it does mean that we must understand the power of our words and know that even the most critical language should be followed by supportive and positive words.

Very few people reading this will believe this applies to them in the extreme. And maybe it doesn't. But each of us has days when we spend much more time dealing with obstacles instead of opportunities, and it is only natural that the accompanying communication can turn negative in a hurry.

Leaders understand the importance of positive, supportive, and uplifting communication. In the midst of turmoil or crisis, people look to their leaders for reassurance and confidence. When they don't find it, they disconnect, disengage, and go into survival mode.

When we find ourselves somewhere short of the effective communicator we would like to be, we should ask ourselves what message we are sending. Are we making our people "flinch" when they see us coming?

We can't change how our message is received unless we change how it is delivered. Make the commitment to increase both the amount and quality of positive and supportive communication with your people. Don't wait until tomorrow or next week to start. Do it right now. Walk out of your office and go to someone and offer a supportive word. If the only time people hear from you is when something is wrong, they will come to dread your communication. In that case, leadership has ceased.

MAKE THE COMMITMENT TO INCREASE BOTH THE
AMOUNT AND QUALITY OF POSITIVE AND SUPPORTIVE
COMMUNICATION WITH YOUR PEOPLE.

You can improve communication by improving your message. Don't fall victim to the tendency in society to focus on the negative. Be the person people want to follow, not avoid. When you do this as the sender in the communication equation, the receivers will respond in kind, and you will again be the effective communicator you know is vital in today's world.

Burning Brightly

CONTINUOUS LEARNING AND LASTING CHANGE

SOMETIMES OUR LIGHT GOES OUT
BUT IS BLOWN INTO FLAME
BY ANOTHER HUMAN BEING.
EACH OF US OWES DEEPEST THANKS
TO THOSE WHO HAVE
REKINDLED THIS LIGHT.

ALBERT SCHWEITZER

A Google a Day...

ONE OF THE TRAITS COMMON to the great leaders of our time, and for all times for that matter, is that they continue to learn throughout their lives and their careers. It is not clear if leaders are more effective because they continually learn, or if they continually learn because they are more effective—or a combination of both.

Either way, there is a clear connection between effective leadership and continually seeking new knowledge. The same goes for effective organizations.

> THERE IS A CLEAR CONNECTION
> BETWEEN EFFECTIVE LEADERSHIP
> AND CONTINUALLY SEEKING
> NEW KNOWLEDGE.

Organizations that continually give their people opportunities for personal and professional growth and development continually outperform those that do not. And this is a philosophy that starts at the top. Leaders have to understand the importance of their own personal life-long learning and the continual learning of everyone within the organization. When both occur, everyone benefits.

How do we create an environment of continual learning and growth both within ourselves and within our organizations?

BUDGET TIME.

Most learning and knowledge sharing will not occur by accident. Much of what we learn by accident is a product of the school of hard knocks. And while this learning method may be effective, it is often not a result of a very positive experience. Budget time out of your personal week for activities that relate to learning something new or expanding a current competency. Also allow time for those who work for you to do the same. When you plan that time into your schedule, it is much more likely to occur.

READ, READ, READ.

There is no better way to learn than to read. Make a goal of reading one new book per month. Then, when you get the hang of it, make it a new book per week. The book doesn't have to be nonfiction, either. While more contemporary issues might be preferable, the act of reading and comprehending in itself is great exercise for your brain and has been shown to make a person sharper in all cognitive activities. Think of reading as lubricating oil for your brain.

WATCH TELEVISION.

We are taught from an early age that we should not get hooked on television. The fact is, with today's cable and satellite choices, a vast amount of information is available through our televisions. From C-SPAN to CNN to the Health Network, knowledge and information have replaced, in many cases, the scandal and intrigue and pure entertainment value of the past couple of decades. TV is a very valid source of information and knowledge. Use it and benefit from it.

A GOOGLE A DAY.

If television has improved its position in the knowledge-delivery business, the Internet has taken over sole possession of the throne as the king of learning. You can find out almost anything you want to know about almost any issue, fact, or person via the Internet. One of the greatest tools available on the Web is the search function. One of the most popular, www.Google.com, can be your roadmap for discovery on almost any topic. One great way to ease your way into the learning mode is to Google each day one subject you would like to know more about. Follow the links Google provides on some subject or person of interest to you, and in a matter of minutes, you can literally become an expert on the issue or person. Again, this is great exercise for your brain and mentally opens you to new knowledge and ideas.

SPEND TIME WITH INTERESTING PEOPLE.

Surround yourself with interesting people who experience interesting things and are willing to discuss them. For instance, if you are interested in overseas travel, you may often find through your local library or service organization a group that routinely discusses their experiences. This also happens every day on the Internet in chat rooms and, now, on blogs. By exchanging information with those who share your interests, you can greatly increase your knowledge and have an enjoyable and stimulating time doing it.

These are just a few suggestions on how we stay active with our learning. It honestly doesn't matter how you do it, as long as you do something. Tests show that individuals who continue to learn and stay mentally active as they age are more effective and live a more productive life. The same goes for organizations.

Effective leaders understand the importance of knowledge and of continually seeking to know more. And by setting a personal example, both in philosophy and in practice, you truly can lead your people into a more productive personal and professional career.

Learning is Key to Improvement

PEOPLE WHO CONTINUE TO LEARN continue to grow. The same is true for organizations. When we examine the traits of the great leaders of our time and throughout history, we find one common practice among them: They continue to read, learn, and expand their brains and skills even after they have achieved considerable greatness. Similarly, high-achieving business organizations like GE, IBM, and Dell invest heavily in technology but even more heavily in their people in the form of continuing education and learning opportunities inside and outside the workplace.

To compete in today's business environment, your organization should have an internal training and education component, even if the training process itself is outsourced. Companies can only stay ahead of the technology and knowledge curves when the people within the company are allowed, encouraged, and even provided incentives to do so.

Effective training in and of itself requires a commitment from the organization as well as the individuals within it. An understanding of the nature of adult learning can go a long way in making sure the investment in time and money provides the greatest return. Following are a few points to help ensure training is effective for you and your organization.

TRAINING CANNOT BE A ONE-TIME EVENT.

Any seminar or conference, no matter how compelling and powerful, will have limited impact if the concepts and outcomes of the training are not reinforced in the workplace. Don't waste your money on sending your employees to outside training and then depend on some miraculous educational intervention. Individual training only works in a supportive organizational environment. And that support includes reinforcing training concepts regularly, either through organizational assets or follow-up by the original education provider.

WORKING ADULTS RELATE BEST
TO LIFE EXPERIENCES.

ADULTS ARE NOT BOOK LEARNERS.

While children, teenagers, and even college students are willing and able to read material and extract the vital points and store them away for future use, adults generally aren't wired that way. Instead, working adults relate best to life experiences. When training concepts can be related to daily occurrences, adults are much more likely to identify with them and put them into practice. Try to avoid textbook or written manual training. Adults are bored by it and simply won't engage. Bring training home and make it applicable to daily life. Theories and adults don't mix; practical ideas that relate to specific work objectives do.

EXPANDING MINDS PRODUCE NEW
AND CREATIVE SOLUTIONS.

Conversely, stagnant minds tend to recycle old solutions. Put simply, it is hard to meet today's and tomorrow's challenges with yesterday's information. Research shows that older adults who continue to learn via reading and other means have stronger cognitive skills later in life. In other words, a brain used is a brain that is sharp. The same goes for our employees. The very act of opening our minds to new ideas provides the kind of mental exercise that spurs new and creative thinking. Then, when we add the new perspective that learning and training can give us, we provide our employees a potential one-two punch that can give your organization the collective edge needed in today's high-competitive marketplace.

Training is no longer just an option for those companies on the leading edge—those that want to get ahead. A viable and effective learning component to our business plan is now a requirement, not a luxury. For those leaders who don't believe they can afford to provide ongoing training, I would submit that you can't afford not to. When we invest in our people, we invest in our future.

One of the most critical roles of any leader is to provide the tools our people need to succeed. None of those tools is more valuable than ongoing education and training. When we allow our people to grow, our organizations grow. Leadership is not a passive task. When we, as leaders, actively encourage our people to expand their minds and continue to learn, we do them, our customers, and ourselves, a favor.

"Yikes and Yea": Using the Past to Map the Future

I SUSPECT YOU KNOW BY NOW MY THOUGHTS about the importance of strategic planning. I believe it is critical that we get away from dealing with today's issues long enough to begin to think about and address tomorrow's challenges and opportunities

Let me be clear. When I talk about strategic planning, I'm not talking about a budget meeting. I'm not talking about some end-of-the-year holiday party during which we count our blessings (that is a good thing, but it's not what I am talking about). I'm not even talking about a get-together in which the owner or CEO stands up in front of managers and decrees what will happen in the next year. No, what I am talking about here is true strategic planning. A day (or more) in which the leadership of the organization gathers, without the daily interruptions of the phone, meetings, and e-mail, ideally at a remote location, a time where today is only a reference point to help us determine where we need to be tomorrow and beyond.

Some companies are very sophisticated in this process. Others are not. Still others have never tried to find out either way. And don't think size is the qualifier here; small companies with just a few employees as well as large corporations with hundreds or thousands of employees can all benefit from strategic thinking and strategic planning.

One of the most effective tools I have seen used in this process is what I call the "Yikes and Yea" tool. While simplistic in its design, this exercise gets to the very heart of what any strategic planning process needs to accomplish. By beginning with "Yikes and Yea" as the first step, the sometimes complex journey to the future seems much more doable.

Quite simply, the idea of this tool is to review the past year and classify your activities and the results of those activities into one of two categories:

1) "Yikes, that turned out badly, and we don't want to do that anymore,"

   or

2) "Yea, that was good. We need to do more of that."

On one extreme, it is simple to get bogged down in all kinds of sophisticated exercises to facilitate strategic planning—so much so that we pedal a great deal but never actually get anywhere. On the other extreme, we can spend valuable time telling war stories and never get around to thinking ahead. Somewhere in between is the desired medium wherein we use the past to map the future.

It is important to know where we went wrong and how to avoid going there again. More importantly, it is critical that we review what has gone right and work to do more of it. Learning from our successes can be so much more valuable than learning from our mistakes.

WHEN HALF THE GROUP INCLUDES
A "YIKES" THAT THE OTHER
HALF CALLS A "YEA," YOU KNOW
ALL THE MUSICIANS ARE NOT PLAYING
OFF THE SAME SONG SHEET.

So, when we aren't sure how to begin the strategic planning process, begin it simply, begin it effectively, and begin it collaboratively by asking each person involved what he or she considers to be the "Yikes and Yeas" of the previous year. This gives you and your organization a great place to start in mapping the path to the future.

This process also helps you determine if your reports are on the same page. When half the group includes a "yikes" that the other half calls a "yea," you know all the musicians are not playing off the same song sheet. When the lists add up and are in general agreement, you can rest assured that your team doesn't need a primer on objectives and priorities and that you can move on to the more important work of strategic planning.

There is nothing more valuable than the input and direction your people can provide your organization. This needs to be done without the daily grind and daily interruptions that come with being in the office. Make the best of your time, and the time of your people, by calling a "time-out" before embarking on the new year, and indulge in some creative and effective strategic thinking and planning. It could prove to be one of the best investments you could ever make.

Creating the Right Environment for Lasting Change

I T GOES BY MANY NAMES: DOWN-SIZING, right-sizing, reengineering, restructuring, turnaround, culture enhancement. Regardless of what you call it, change is difficult. Creating lasting change for the better is even more difficult, and getting it right the first time is darn near impossible.

Notice I said "darn near." The fact is, change is a process that begins before it even begins. One of the ways we get change right the first time is to create an environment that allows for change. This environment is not about your building or other capital investments. It's not about how much money is spent in the process. It is about creating a mindset that will allow for the technology or the new idea to take hold from within each person in the organization. In short, lasting change does not occur by proclamation.

So, how do we get it right before we ever get started? There are a number of mistakes leaders make when they begin the change process. By avoiding these mistakes, we can "darn near" ensure we have the right environment for lasting change. They include:

NOT CREATING A SENSE OF URGENCY FOR CHANGE.

To get our people on the road to change, they have to understand why. When we first mention change, the first reaction of most people is, "What is wrong with the way we are doing it now?" You must be prepared and willing to answer this question without placing blame. When people in the organization can contemplate change without feeling threatened or "blamed," they are much more likely to embrace it. When you help your people understand why change is needed, in clear and businesslike terms, you begin to create an environment for lasting change.

CHANGE HAS TO BUILD LIKE A
WILDFIRE—IT STARTS WITH A SINGLE
FLAME OR SPARK AND IMMEDIATELY
BUILDS MOMENTUM BY SPREADING.

NOT BUILDING A COALITION FOR CHANGE.

Any effective initiative needs champions; leaders can't make it happen alone. When management uses the "because I said so, and I'm the boss" method, change will last only as long as managers are in the room. Change has to build like a wildfire—it starts with a single flame or spark and immediately builds momentum by spreading. Igniting several sparks within the organization by identifying champions in various departments can help the fire spread exponentially quicker. It is more dependable, because one spark that fails to catch does not doom the process.

NOT CREATING A VISION FOR CHANGE.

Just as our people have to know why we are changing *from* something, they need to understand what we are moving *towards*. One of the top priorities of any leader should be to provide a vision of the preferred outcome, a glimpse of the light at the end of the tunnel, so that people in the organization know what they are striving for as opposed to what they are trying to escape. Where do we want our organization and our people to be when we have "succeeded?" The leader has to be willing and able to provide that vision.

NOT PERSONALIZING THE CHANGE.

"What's in it for me?" Every human being has asked this question at some point in his or her life. Leaders must personalize change in a way that a) helps people understand what is "in it for them" so they internalize the effort; and b) identifies the individual's role in achieving "success." We often talk about team objectives and goals, but we don't drill down to the level where all individuals understand what they could and should do. Leaders should be able to provide individual objectives for members of the team. If you can't drill down to that level, how can you expect them to do it on their own? A few highly motivated folks might get it independently. But most won't.

The success or failure of a change initiative depends a great deal on what happens in the beginning, even more so than what happens in the end. Some say, "All's well that ends well," but great leaders know that "What begins well, ends well."

By spending the time and effort to create an environment that supports and nurtures change at the beginning of the process, we can save a great deal of time and effort along the way and "darn near" guarantee our chances of creating lasting change in our organizations.

Living What You Learn Will Make It Last

O NE OF THE ISSUES I AM CONSTANTLY quizzed about is how we can take the inspiration and excitement that result from a leadership conference and make them last once we are back in the day-to-day world that drove us to find answers in the first place. "How can I use this information to create change in my company?"

The truth is, one of our greatest challenges as leaders is to take the inspiration in our lives, regardless of where it comes from, and make it part of who we are and what we stand for. Inspiration, which by definition comes from an external source, becomes motivation when we apply it and internalize it. Only when we have embraced the inspiration can we pass it on to others.

INSPIRATION, WHICH BY DEFINITION
COMES FROM AN EXTERNAL SOURCE,
BECOMES MOTIVATION WHEN WE
APPLY IT AND INTERNALIZE IT.

To know *without* doing is temporary. You can be inspired and emboldened by something you learn or experience, but the only way to truly know it is to apply it and to pass it on to others. To know by doing is what creates commitment.

So how, in a more practical way, can we take new skills and knowledge we acquire at something like a leadership conference and create a change that lasts, both in ourselves and in others? Here are a few ideas:

REMEMBER PERSPECTIVE.

You may come back fired up from an event or conference, but others have been at the office in the very environment you are seeking to change. Understand that others may not be quite as excited and inspired as you are, so be gentle. Don't bombard those around you with your new ideas and knowledge all at one time. Develop a plan to share your excitement with others in a methodical and respectful way.

DEVELOP A PLAN.

People can only take so much good news. Review what part of the new knowledge or skills has the most potential to positively impact your organization. As with everything in life, it is important to prioritize. Determine what can have the most impact for your people, and lay out exactly how and when you will communicate it to others. A step-by-step process, call it a lesson plan, can provide you with the measured and consistent delivery method needed to begin to inspire others in the same way you have been inspired.

SAY IT AND DO IT.

By applying what you have learned and what excites you, you become part of the change you seek to create. The best way to ensure you remain excited and motivated is to live the things that you have learned and then pass them on to others. It is critical to remember that, as a leader, you have to set the example. Don't pick and choose which parts you will apply to yourself. When your people see your excitement and your motivation, they are much more likely to adopt the new knowledge or tools themselves. However, if they perceive that you are pushing concepts on them that you are not willing to adhere to, they will not buy in. Don't let your actions speak louder than your memos. Don't just talk the talk—walk the walk.

REWARD WHAT MATTERS.

It is critical to remember that what gets rewarded, gets done. If you have new ideas you want to take hold in your organization, it can be very effective to provide incentives for the behavior you seek. This should be part of the plan discussed above. Lay out the new concept, consistently reinforce the concept, and measure results, provide feedback, and reward appropriate behavior.

Real change takes time. While you may be inspired by something you heard or saw one time, even you will need to convert the inspiration into motivation and commitment. Don't expect miracles, and don't expect everyone to get as excited as you are. More importantly, be consistent. By knowing what is most important and continually reinforcing those issues, you have the best chance of spreading the excitement you are experiencing.

Leaders inspire others. Leaders provide a vision of the preferred outcome. And probably most importantly, leaders set the example. When you want others to be as excited as you are, be realistic, be consistent, and be patient. Real change takes time. Take what you learn, put it into action, and pass it on to others. By doing so, you have the best opportunity to create change that lasts, both in yourself and in your people.

Luminaries on the Path

REMEMBER TO ENJOY THE JOURNEY

WHAT YOU LEAVE BEHIND IS
NOT WHAT IS ENGRAVED IN STONE
MONUMENTS, BUT WHAT IS WOVEN
INTO THE LIVES OF OTHERS.

PERICLES

Understanding the Rat Race

LILY TOMLIN ONCE SAID, "The only problem with being in a rat race is that even if you win the race, you're still a rat." Wow! Those are some pretty deep words to think about.

We all find ourselves in the "rat race" from time to time, some more so than others. Many of us have come to the conclusion that the "rat race" is just part of the game, and we have to learn how to compete. That being said, there is a real danger that we are creating a "rat race" mentality in our own lives and in our own organizations by the actions we take—and, sometimes, by those we refuse to take.

I have heard many discussions about those people in life who are always working to get "somewhere." They are so intent on getting "there," wherever "there" is, that they spend their whole lives trying to get "there" and either they never do or, when they do get "there," they are too old or burned out to enjoy it.

The key, many believe, is to enjoy the journey as much as the destination. Why? Because we will spend much more time on the journey than we are likely to spend at the destination. I am reminded of bus trips my grandmother used to make from Texas back to her former home in California. When she returned, she very seldom talked about California, but she would always talk about how beautiful the trip was. She would expound on the beauty of the Painted Desert and the Grand Canyon, about the long, winding roads through the West, and the beautiful sunsets each evening as she traveled.

THE KEY IS TO ENJOY THE JOURNEY
AS MUCH AS THE DESTINATION.

I know for a fact she enjoyed the destination, but she also knew the importance of enjoying the journey. We often talk about how leaders must help craft a vision, a preferred outcome, and how they should have clear objectives and goals. But these are all destinations. What are we doing to help our people enjoy the journey? Truly enlightened leaders know that our people have to get up every day and be part of a journey. These same leaders are putting as much emphasis on making the journey enjoyable as they are on making the destination fulfilling and even profitable.

How can we, as leaders, help our people enjoy the journey while striving every day for those important destinations? Here are a few ideas.

ACKNOWLEDGE THE PROCESS.
We spend ninety days producing quarterly financial results that are released on one day. And then we start all over again. Another ninety days, quarterly results, and then we start over yet again. The cycle never changes. In a year, we spend 365 days producing results that, at some level, only matter four days out of the year. Obviously, financial results have a more lasting impact. But when we spend ninety days on a journey to get to a destination, and then spend one day, or even less, with the results, and then start over again, it is critical that we understand that the journey is far more important to our people's morale and well-being than the destination. All this is to say that we can put too much emphasis on results (destination) and not nearly enough emphasis on the process (journey)…and we often do. More focus on the former will almost always convert to better news on the latter.

UNDERSTAND WHAT DRIVES YOUR PEOPLE.
You may well be driven by financial results and profitability. But the truth is, many of the people in your organization may not be. They are often more

motivated, or de-motivated in some cases, by their daily working conditions and environment. They often have friendships with those they work with. They have family issues they are thinking about while they are working for you. They are thinking about making it to their son's baseball game or their daughter's dance lessons or what they have to pick up at the grocery store on the way home. When you spend every day talking about goals and objectives, you can actually turn people off to them, because the people may be more concerned about that particular day in their life. Again, there should be a balance between the present (the journey) and the future (the destination).

HELP YOURSELF.

While all this is important to your people, it is critically important to your leadership health. You can't run the rat race in your mind (How are we going to make budget? How are we going to hit plan?) and simply turn that off when it comes to dealing with your people and being a good listener and leader. As Lily Tomlin warned us, we don't want to win the race and still be a rat. From time to time, stop the race in your head. Not just at home, but at work as well. It is very important for each of us to enjoy the journey and not just focus constantly on the destination. Again, balance is important.

You will always hear me talk about the importance of goals and objectives. But the process of how to reach them is just as, if not more, important. One without the other makes both senseless.

So, the next time you feel as if you are caught up in the rat race, do something about it. There is nothing to be gained by being so focused on the destination that you fail to enjoy the journey. Stop and smell the roses. They truly are worth the little bit of time it takes in the overall scheme of things.

Watch Out for Those Ruts!

WE OFTEN GET UP EACH DAY and deal with many of the same issues we dealt with the day before, and the day before that, and the...well, you get the point. This can be quite challenging. As leaders, part of our job is to inspire others. But often, a more appropriate question is, "How do we inspire ourselves?" How do we get over that hump that sometimes comes when we get into a rut and become frustrated or bored with what we do?

This may not happen to you often. Then again, it may happen more than you want to admit. Either way, it is important to know how to pull yourself out of the ditch. If you wait for that tow truck to show up (in the form of another person) to do it for you, you may be waiting a long time.

Following are a few tips that may help you pull yourself out of that funk that could be holding you back:

GET OUT OF YOUR OFFICE.

Often, when times are difficult and people are frustrated, they make the mistake of isolating themselves, both physically and emotionally. In fact, the best thing you can do is to get out amongst the bright people that work for and with you and let them re-energize you. Just a note: if your people are the problem and the reason you are in a rut, do something about it. As I have said many times, procrastination is the greatest enemy to leadership. Not making the hard decisions in a timely manner can drive you straight into the ditch, and you often can't get out until you face these issues head-on.

> THE BEST THING YOU CAN DO IS TO
> GET OUT AMONGST THE BRIGHT PEOPLE
> THAT WORK FOR AND WITH YOU AND
> LET THEM RE-ENERGIZE YOU.

WORK SMARTER, NOT HARDER.

When we feel we are falling behind, we often make the mistake of thinking the answer is to pedal harder. In fact, the real answer is to pedal smarter. Make a list of the activities that are bogging you down, both time-wise and emotionally, and spend thirty minutes or an hour figuring out a plan to address these issues by working smarter, not harder. There is nothing more frustrating than ending the day feeling as though you didn't make any progress. Most of us simply run out of hours in the day to get things done. Remember, you are judged not by what you do but by what you get done.

MAKE A PURCHASE AT THE EMOTIONAL GAS STATION.

Sometimes, we just need to relax and recharge. That is often hard to do in the very environment that is dragging us down. Don't wait until three or four people tell you that you look like you need a vacation. By that time, you have already negatively impacted the organization. Get away—whatever that means to you. Whether it is for an hour or a week, go do something that refills your tank emotionally. The sooner you get away, the sooner you can recharge and get back. And by the way, if you don't want to get back to what you are doing, you really do need a break—or another job!

It is very difficult to inspire others if you yourself are not inspired. Take care of yourself before you worry about taking care of others. The next time you feel yourself in a rut, do something about it. In parts of northern Canada where unpaved roads stay frozen much of the year, the summer thaw often produces deep tire ruts. Signs along the roads warn drivers to be cautious about the ruts they get into, as they may be in them for a while.

The same goes for us. Often, the only way we can recover is to rescue ourselves. Make sure you are doing what needs to be done to keep your emotional fuel tank full, and you will be much better at helping those around you do the same.

Live Your Dreams,
Act on Your Desires

I N MY EARLY CAREER AS A JOURNALIST, I had the opportunity to write about a wide variety of compelling topics, ranging from the savings and loan scandals of the '80s to the final bowl game of legendary Alabama coach Paul "Bear" Bryant, to the almost unthinkable death of five children in a tragic house fire.

But like almost every cub reporter, I spent my first few months writing death notices, more commonly known as obituaries. In addition to the day-to-day reporting of deaths in the community, I was responsible for "pre-writing" obituaries of important people in town, such as the mayor, city council members, business leaders, etc. The theory was that, if one of these people were to suddenly die, we would need to have the information "in the can" so that we could run the story without having to do a great deal of research.

I recall one local leader about whom I had pre-written an obituary. He did not die while I was still working at the newspaper, but he did perish in a car accident several years later. In all, twelve years had passed since I had pre-written his death notice. I read the front-page story of his untimely death and noticed not much had changed with him since I had researched his life. In fact, upon closer review, I determined nothing had changed in those twelve years; it was the exact same information I had written more than a decade earlier.

In retrospect, I would hate to think that could be me, that more than ten years of my life could pass with no significant changes or accomplishments. This is proof positive that we shouldn't wait to do what we know needs to be done. The truth is, if we wait, we may never get the opportunity.

I'm going to ask you now to do an activity I've done in some of my leadership sessions. I ask participants to write their own death notices, assuming they live a full and fruitful life. In other words, what do you expect to accomplish in your life, and what mark do you expect to leave on this Earth and the people around you? Then, as a second step, write the obituary as if you died today. What have you accomplished to this point in your life?

WHAT DO YOU EXPECT TO ACCOMPLISH
IN YOUR LIFE, AND WHAT MARK DO
YOU EXPECT TO LEAVE ON THIS EARTH
AND THE PEOPLE AROUND YOU?

Now, compare the two. What do you want to ultimately accomplish or be known for that you have yet to fulfill? What is still on your agenda that has not been covered? What do you want to be when you grow up?

While this exercise might seem a bit morbid, it simply helps illustrate that we have to make the best use of our time every single day. All these things we say we will do when we have time may never happen, because we may never have the time. We can get so busy living our lives that we forget to live our lives.

I have talked about the importance of reducing, if not eliminating, procrastination from our lives. We very often know what needs to be done, yet we don't always take the final step of pulling the trigger and acting on what we know. By waiting until "the time is right," we can very often procrastinate our way right into potential failure. Do what needs to be done when it needs to be done.

Great leaders know the importance of acting on good information, with good instincts, and with solid preparation. However, you can always justify your way into waiting. No matter how motivated you are to act, you can always find an excuse to wait.

Whether or not you go to the extreme of writing your own ultimate death notice, you should at least realize that life truly does have to be led one day at a time. We should work to accomplish all we can, in a reasonable fashion, each and every day with the full understanding we may never get another chance. If there is something about ourselves we want to change, something we want to accomplish, something we want to be known for, we should be working on it today. We may not accomplish it, but at least we can make progress on it.

Don't look up ten years from now and figure out you wanted to accomplish so many things that you just never got to. You owe it to yourself and to the people around you to act on your own hopes and desires. If you live your life outwardly as you dream it inwardly, you will find there is little distance between where you are and where you want to be.

Don't Wait for a Tragedy

I T NEVER CEASES TO AMAZE AND UPLIFT ME how the people of this country respond to a tragedy. Whether it is a hurricane or a terrorist attack on our own shores, or an earthquake or tsunami on another continent, the people of America consistently rise to the occasion in so many ways.

After 9/11, it was easy to see a change in people—people you may not even have known. The roughness that comes from everyday business and personal challenges simply fades away for a period. Instances of aggressive driving reduce. People are more likely to hold the door open for you. And church? Following 9/11, churches and synagogues were packed to the rafters.

Then there is the financial support. The money raised for the victims of 9/11, for the victims of the Indonesian tsunami, and for the Gulf Coast hurricanes totaled in the hundreds of billions of dollars. In the wake of Hurricane Katrina, individuals, families, and entire communities opened their homes to total strangers. The instances of generosity and selflessness were literally breathtaking.

Every time the call goes out, and often when it doesn't, we respond and rise to the occasion. We put aside the petty issues that on a normal day drag us down or lead to an argument or confrontation. We tend to put everything into perspective following a tragedy that brings us all together.

I just wonder why it has to take a tragedy to bring out the best in us? I have to ask why it is necessary for us to face a brush with death or some other life-changing experience to change our perspective—the way we look at our situation and deal with others. Wouldn't it make for a much better world if we all operated in some enlightened way every day, the way we did for a few weeks after 9/11?

Following are a few ideas that might help each of us maintain a more positive attitude, cultivate a more giving nature, and be more forgiving of the things in others that, on a normal day, might irritate or bother us.

DON'T DROWN IN YOUR OWN "TO-DO" LIST.

We often start the day facing a hefty list of things that have to get done. Unfortunately, these lists are often full of problems we have to overcome. The list should be called the "problems I haven't gotten to yet" list. When we begin the day with a mountain of problems in front of us, it is very difficult to maintain a positive attitude.

TAKE STOCK OF ALL AROUND YOU THAT IS GOOD.

When we constantly face what is wrong, we often don't give ourselves the opportunity to enjoy all that is good around us. I heard one of the survivors of the 9/11 attack say he began to count his blessings every day after he survived the fire and tower collapse. Why wait to count your blessings? If we begin each and every day counting our blessings, we have a better chance to put ourselves in the right frame of mind.

> MAKE A DECISION TO DO SOMETHING
> YOU HAVE BEEN MEANING TO DO
> AT LEAST ONCE A WEEK.

MAKE A DECISION TO MAKE A DIFFERENCE.

It sounds like a cliché, but it is true that our psyche needs to know we are making a difference with what we do. We are often so busy doing "what it is we do" that we get to the end of the day and never got around to "what we meant to do." Make a decision to do something you have been meaning to do at least once a week. Make that call to a friend or relative just to see how they are doing. Visit your child or grandchild's school. Volunteer an hour of your time at a shelter or a library or a senior center. Or maybe go home and do that project you have been putting off for weeks or months or even years. Whatever it means in your book, make a difference outside your work.

NEVER FORGET.

Most of us remember where we were when we first saw the planes fly into the World Trade Center. Many of us remember the feeling in our stomachs when we figured out what was really happening that day in Manhattan. And it is very difficult to forget the funerals of those who died in the attacks. The next time you get upset over something small—something minor in the overall scheme of things—remember what really matters. When we keep things in perspective, we are more valuable to the organization, to those around us, and to ourselves. No one wants to dwell on tragedy. However, we can't afford to forget, for all kinds of reasons. But the main reason is that we need to understand what is important. When we can keep that enlightened perspective, we become less encumbered by the little things that happen in our day and, often, the day of those with whom we interact.

You are the only one who can control your own attitude. You can't change others; you can only change yourself. If each of us who responds so compassionately and selflessly in the wake of a tragedy could find it in ourselves to carry that attitude into each and every day, our world would be a better place. And ultimately, when we lead with compassion and selflessness, we are more effective in most everything we do.

Don't wait until you are touched by a tragedy or a near-death experience to live your life the way you have always wanted. If you are perfectly happy with your attitude, the way you deal with others, and what you accomplish, congratulations. This chapter was not for you. For the rest of us, we can do better—and we should start today. Don't wait until tomorrow to share the kindness that is deep in your heart today.

Being Remembered for What Matters

WHO WAS THE CEO OF THE U.S.-BASED company that in 2004 provided the greatest return on investment to its shareholders? Who was the Most Valuable Player in the 2002 World Series? Who won the 1992 U.S. Open golf tournament?

Without help or research, I doubt that many of us could answer these questions. However, what about these next questions?

Who was the coach of your child's little league team last year? What teacher from your school days had the most positive impact on your life? What is the name of the person you most enjoy spending time with?

Most all of us could readily answer these questions. Yet somehow, it seems we spend more time trying to become the answer to one of the first three questions than one of the latter three. Many folks want to be known for something. There is nothing wrong with that. But *that* we are known is not the issue; it's *what* we are known for that is important. Often what we seek is more about title, about status, about stature, even about winning. But where does status really come from? What does it mean to win?

As leaders, we need to understand our role. When we focus on winning, we miss the point. What we should be doing is helping our people win, and in turn they will make us winners. If profitability is the goal, the task should be to take care of our people. Our people will take care of our customers, then our customers will provide the revenue we need to be profitable. Yet, we often spend more time managing profitability than leading our people.

I have asked the question before, "Are we paying attention to the right things?" Are we applying our focus to the areas where that focus is not only most needed but also the best utilized? In many cases, the answer is no.

We have to stop and ask ourselves questions such as:

- What am I focused on? (Remember, whatever we focus on we get more of, even if it is negative.)

- Am I making the best use of my time?

- Am I providing the appropriate amount of support to my people?

- Do I have the correct balance between fire fighting and fire prevention?

- Am I running my business or department, or is it running me?

As leaders, what we should be known for is providing our people with the following:

- A clear vision of the preferred outcome;

- The tools needed to achieve the vision;

- The encouragement and inspiration for our people to achieve at a very high level.

What are you known for? Great leaders are not known for winning. They aren't known for the destination—they are known for the journey. I have never heard anyone say they admired General George Patton because he won a particular battle. It is how he went about his role as a general that he is known for. His people believed in him, had faith in him, trusted him, and would follow him onto almost any battlefield.

Country music star George Strait in his hit song "You'll Be There" has a line that says, "I've never seen a hearse with a luggage rack." What we will be known for is what we do along the way, not where we finish.

WHAT WE WILL BE KNOWN FOR
IS WHAT WE DO ALONG THE WAY,
NOT WHERE WE FINISH.

The next time you are sitting in your office or driving in your car, trying to figure out what issues to tackle next, think about what your role really is. Think about what you can do to have the most impact on your people and your organization. Think about how your time and talents are best utilized. Think about what you really want to be known for. When you look at life with this kind of perspective, you truly are thinking as a leader.